A DAY FOR DANCING

The Life and Music of Lloyd Pfautsch

Kenneth W. Hart

Number 9 in the North Texas Lives of Musicians Series

University of North Texas Press

Denton, Texas

10 9 8 7 6 5 4 3 2 1

Permissions:
University of North Texas Press
1155 Union Circle #311336
Denton, TX 76203-5017

The paper used in this book meets the minimum requirements of the American National Standard for Permanence of Paper for Printed Library Materials, z39.48.1984. Binding materials have been chosen for durability.

Library of Congress Cataloging-in-Publication Data

Hart, Kenneth W., 1939–
A day for dancing : the life and music of Lloyd Pfautsch / Kenneth W. Hart.
pages cm — (Number 9 in the North Texas lives of musicians series)
Includes bibliographical references and index.

ISBN 978-1-57441-567-4 (cloth : alk. paper) — ISBN 978-1-57441-581-0 (ebook)
1. Pfautsch, Lloyd. 2. Composers—Texas—Dallas—Biography. 3. Choral conductors—Texas—Dallas—Biography. 4. College teachers—Texas—Dallas—Biography. I. Title. II. Series: North Texas lives of musicians series ; no. 9.
ML410.P3156H37 2014
782.0092—dc23
[B]
2014026271

A Day for Dancing: The Life and Music of Lloyd Pfautsch is
Number 9 in the North Texas Lives of Musicians Series

The electronic edition of this book was made possible by
the support of the Vick Family Foundation.

Dedication

To Ellen, my wife and my best friend

Contents

List of Musical Examples

You can listen to performances of some of these pieces, some conducted by Lloyd Pfautsch, at http://digital.library.unt.edu/ark:/67531/metadc335333/

1. "Camp Song," 1943, unpublished manuscript

2. *Requiem Mass*, c. 1945, unpublished manuscript

3. "*Puer nobis*," 1953, C.C. Birchard & Co. #1615

4. "Israel at the Red Sea," 1946 manuscript (published by Lawson-Gould in 1991)

5. *Five Narrative Carols* (I. "Adam lay ybounden"), 1953 (published by C. C. Birchard)

6a. Brahms *Leibeslieder Waltz* No. 1, C. F. Peters edition
6b. *Songs My Grossmama Sang* (I. "Fraulein Bo-Peepen") Lawson-Gould #546

7. *The Lord is my Shepherd*, 1957, Summy-Birchard #492-12032

8. "Sing Praise to God," 1959, Fred Bock (1988 edition of 1959 Summy-Birchard publication) #BG2037

9. "Seek to Serve," 1983, Agape Press #AMP003

10. "Sing Praises," 1967, Lawson-Gould #51367

11. *A Day for Dancing*, 1969, Lawson-Gould #51475

12a. "*Omnis spiritus laudet Dominum*," 1973, Lawson-Gould #51802
12b. Performance Directions for "*Omnis spiritus laudet Dominum*"

13. "Go and Tell John," unpublished manuscript of Pfautsch's TTBB arrangement

14. "I wonder why?" 1972, Agape Press, Hope Publishing #AG7104

15. "Let us praise Creation's Lord!" 1979, Hope Publishing #LP3715

16. "Lord Jesus, Think on Me," 1997, Abingdon Press #061881

Acknowledgments

I am first of all greatly indebted to Lloyd and Edie Pfautsch for their friendship, their support, and their collegial treatment of Ellen and me. Next I appreciate the lengthy and constant support of my immediate family: Ellen, Justin, and Daniel Hart as well as Stephanie Patsley Hart and Rachel Ballard.

To detail their kindnesses and assistance would be too lengthy for the space allotted, but they know what those contributions were and I hope they know how much I appreciate and love them. I am grateful to Perkins School of Theology at Southern Methodist University, William Lawrence, Dean, for granting me a sabbatical leave in the Spring of 2000 to accomplish the initial research for this project. The encouragement and staff support were extremely generous, particularly the tape transcriptions prepared by Ann Ralston. David Kravig-Williams kindly offered technical assistance whenever needed. I am, of course indebted to those who allowed me to tape interviews with them: Jane Marshall, Carlton "Sam" Young, Alice Parker, Robert Anderson, and Walter Gould. Several former students assisted as well, especially David Collett, Kenton Kravig-Williams, and Robert Brooks. Beyond that I am grateful to Dr. Karen DeVinney, Assistant Director/Managing Editor at UNT Press. She guided and supported this project for a very long time and deserves much of the credit for the final results.

The Call to Dance

A Prologue

It was 27 June 1965 and the venue was the 13,000-seat San Francisco Cow Palace, a gargantuan site, home to national rodeos, Ringling Brothers, Barnum and Bailey circuses, and numerous major sporting events. The six-acre building had been the embarkation site for thousands of troops involved in World War II (1941–46). But ironically today's festival was being held for virtually the opposite purpose: the Convocation of Religion for World Peace, a part of the observance of the twentieth anniversary of the United Nations. At one end was seated a massed choir from area churches, temples, synagogues, and other houses of worship numbering 2,000 musicians. They were accompanied by the esteemed Sixth Army Brass Band. Surrounding them in the nearly full house were many of the world leaders who were delegates to the United Nations, including Secretary General U Tant. The rest of the "congregation" was comprised of worshippers from the widest range of faiths: Catholics, Protestants, Jews, Hindus, Buddhists, Muslims, and Eastern Orthodox Christians, all gathered in support of a common cause: world peace. The musical maestro for this momentous gathering was a lanky, bald-headed, renowned conductor from Dallas, Texas, by the name of Lloyd Pfautsch. Clearly at the pinnacle of his career, the forty-four-year old was selected for this prestigious assignment in recognition of his stature as one of the top choral musicians in the United States. The only other such gathering had been at the UN's tenth anniversary celebration (The Festival of Faith) in the same venue and the conductor for that convocation had been Pfautsch's friend and mentor, Robert Shaw, also chosen because he was the best among his peers.

The amiable professor from Southern Methodist University acquitted himself so well on this occasion that he received accolades from around the country for nearly a year afterwards. His already busy schedule of guest conducting appearances and choral workshop invitations literally burgeoned beyond his availability for several seasons after this event.

Pfautsch was allowed only three rehearsals with the enormous choir (one on Friday with half the group, a second on Saturday with the other half and only one on Sunday with the entire choir and the brass.) But the precise diction, uniform vowel colors, and tight ensemble achieved through precision conducting gestures, all trademarks of Pfautsch's success, were enough to create a musical ensemble that was at once easy to understand and exciting to hear. He brought to the table the results of all of his years of study, struggle, analysis, and experience and applied these hard-won skills in the most intense of situations with the ease of a master, bolstering his already growing reputation as an icon of American choral music.

His comment ever afterward was "Well, it was a lot of fun. They had everything so well organized, including feeding 2,000 people a barbeque dinner behind stage in only an hour's time. All I had to do was just think about the scores and conduct them. It was a treat." This humble attitude was very much a part of the Pfautsch persona and was one of his many endearing qualities. Others included an infectious sense of humor, a clear understanding of right and wrong, an impeccable sense of integrity, and an abiding belief in preparation and hard work.

But no one achieves such recognition and success overnight. Pfautsch had been struggling, studying, working, and performing for forty-one years in order to successfully arrive at this high point in his career. It began when at the age of three he sang a solo for his church's Christmas pageant and realized that being on stage was nothing to fear and was, in fact, a lot of fun! As Pfautsch recalled: "I never regarded music as a vocation, but rather an avocation, until I had already completed graduate work in Theology at Union Theological Seminary in New York City." Only at that stage, at the age of twenty-five, was he finally able to acknowledge that music was his calling and that he would have to work hard to catch up to those who had figured it out much earlier in their careers. So he stayed at Union for a Master of Sacred Music degree, to which he was admitted by exception (his Bachelor's degree was not in Music.) He continued his already successful singing career (having sung under Wilhousky, Toscanini, and Robert Shaw), learned as much about conducting as he could (he even organized his fellow students to petition the administration at Union to offer better conducting instruction) and began his lifelong passion for composing. His composition teacher, Harold Friedell, immediately recognized his talent and arranged for the Union Seminary Choir to perform one of his works in a public venue.

Ten years as Director of Choral Activities at Illinois Wesleyan University, one at the University of Illinois, and six years at Southern Methodist University as Director of Choral Activities had helped him prepare to succeed in San Francisco. Numerous appearances as guest conductor at All-State High School Choral Festivals and intergenerational festivals held by multi-church choirs throughout the country had seasoned him as well.

In Lloyd Pfautsch's mind his San Francisco appearance was the most important single engagement he ever performed. He rather shyly asked one day if it could be featured in the Prologue to this biography! In truth, though, his career continued to flourish and his fame grew ever greater from that event until near the end of his life. In spite of this he remained a very modest man. When this writer first approached him about doing a book on his life and music he was quite hesitant about it. Only our friendship convinced him to agree. At our first interview session, however, he apologized for his initial reactions saying: "I hope you didn't think that I was being vain in trying to discourage you. I really appreciate your interest in doing this project. It floored me; that's the thing of it. I never thought of myself as that important that somebody would want to do a biography."

His compositions were so popular and practical that nearly every important church and academic choral library in the country included his works among their repertoire. His story is a fascinating one that, were it fiction, would be classified as suitable for General Audiences and almost Pollyanna-like in its message: if you work hard and behave ethically and morally you will have a happy and fulfilling life. His life was just that, full of fun and rewards for doing what he considered "the right thing to do." He also had an enduring sense of humor that got him through the hard times. Further, he was lucky enough to find a mate for life, Edie, who was also an outstanding musician with similar Midwestern ideals and principles. Luckily she had the capacity to be a great mother and a wonderfully supportive wife as well. She helped him get through the challenges he faced.

Pfautsch's life was an enviable one in many respects, but certainly not an easy one. He achieved a great deal more than most of us can expect to, but it was always through hard work and the ability to maintain his considerable sense of humor while meeting each challenge head on. Like most of us, Pfautsch led a bittersweet life, largely happy and satisfying but full of unexpected twists and turns, some very difficult, even painful and some serendipitous. The fruits of his labor are woven inextricably into the fabric of American choral music throughout the second half of the twentieth century. As singer, conductor, educator, and composer he had few peers. His contributions are both legion and long-lasting. He will not soon vanish from our collective memory.

Chapter 1

The Dance of Prophecy

(Missouri and Illinois)

On October 2, 1827, Joseph Pfautsch, a successful, thirty-two-year-old master barrel-maker from Austria, was betrothed to Margaretha Hoermann, a twenty-seven-year-old farmer's daughter from Altmuenster, Bavaria.[1] They were married at the Catholic church in the tiny town of Maineck (population 200) in the upper Franconia district. The Pfautsches were married for eleven years before Margaretha gave birth to a son, Johann, in 1838.[2] Soon after, they decided to move to Missouri, along with Joseph's brother and his family. Like many Germans the couples had been charmed by the writings of Gottfried Duden, a German who lived in that part of the New World in the late 1820s and wrote to his friends and relatives back in Europe about the beauty of the Missouri Valley.[3] Its similarities to the Rhineland and its opportunities for prosperity made it attractive to many German immigrants. The Pfautsches settled in the largely German community of Hermann, about sixty miles west of St. Louis. Young Johann, like his father Joseph, worked hard. He eventually saved enough money that he and a partner were able to build a concert hall in Hermann, replete with café and *bierstube*. His auditorium was a hub of social and cultural activity. In recent years the building has been declared an official historic building and, like much of the original downtown Hermann, is being restored.

In 1864, the twenty-six-year-old entrepreneur married Catherina Weinert. She bore him three sons before she died. After a period of grieving, Johann once more fell in love at the age of forty-three, this time with Emelie Preus, twenty-one years his junior. Either because it was his second marriage or because Emelie was a Protestant, their 1881 ceremony was performed in the priest's house, not in the church. Three years later they were blessed with a son, Walter.

Unfortunately Johann Pfautsch died less than four years after the birth of his son Walter. So the young Walter not only spent his youth without a father, he also had to quit school early to work and help support his family. For some reason Johann's business partner did not give his widow any share in the concert hall after her husband's death and so the family had to start anew with virtually no funds to help support them. Walter eventually built a career as an insurance salesman. He married Frieda Puchta in 1911 and they had a child, Walter Jr., in 1913, but Frieda died in the influenza epidemic that swept across the United States during World War I. After the war, Walter, like his father before him, decided to remarry. He chose Ouida Henselmeier from St. Louis and in 1919 settled in the nearby town of Washington, as foreman at the still-famous Meerschaum Pipe Factory. He looked upon this job as more stable than that of salesman in the still infant insurance business. Also, he was offered some shares of the company stock as part of his initial benefits. Walter and Ouida had two children: Lloyd (1921) and Marian (1924). The family always regarded all three children as equal members of the family and Lloyd, for instance, did not even know Walter was a half-brother until late grade-school days, when a classmate told him as a way to tease him ("I know something you don't know." "No you don't!" "Yes, I do!". . .)

Both Walter Jr., and Marian Pfautsch showed promise in the field of business, following in their father's career path to some extent. Walter became a jeweler and jewelry store owner in Sullivan, Missouri. Marian rose to the position of vice president in a building and loan association in Washington. But a different career path was intended for Lloyd.

The Pfautsches were devout Christians. No longer Catholics after Johann's death, they were very active in the local Evangelical and Reformed Church, a Protestant amalgam brought to the United States from northern Germany where the Kaiser had decreed that the Lutheran and the Reformed Churches would unite into the Evangelical Church of Prussia. Lloyd recalled the wonderful singing of the congregation. "Although some had raucous voices none had inhibitions at all about cutting loose and singing the hymns and chorales."[4] While most worship services were conducted in English at the Washington E & R Church, the pastor was bilingual and once a month a service in German was offered as well. Lloyd grew up hearing the best of German sacred music as the norm. Later in life he was shocked to find in the large New York City churches that most members of the congregation, especially the men, did not even try to sing during the service. Because of his dedication to the church and probably because of his interests and aptitudes Walter and Ouida determined that the entrepreneurial world was not for Lloyd. He, they decided, should be a minister in the Evangelical and Reformed Church. All of his post-secondary education was directed toward that goal. All of it, that is, until he himself realized in the midst of his graduate studies that he actually had a slightly different calling to a slightly different ministry. More of that later.

Growing up in Washington, Missouri, in the 1920s and '30s was a largely pleasant experience for the Pfautsch children, although Lloyd did recall that there was a lot of prejudice, which is sometimes more noticeable in small towns. Because of the anti-German feelings after World War I and even more so after World War II, there was no German taught in the public schools of Washington when Lloyd was a student. German had been offered in the schools when his father was a youth, but no longer by Lloyd's time, even though there was a very large German population in the town. He remembered his father's lengthy talks in German with his grandmother when she came to visit. He sadly recalled that a fine cabinet-maker of German descent was forced to leave town because of gossip that he might be a spy. The Pfautsch family was not a part of that action and they felt badly that it had happened in their town. Lloyd remembered his father working hard in the pipe factory by day, proud of the large number of pipes that were produced and shipped around the world, especially to Europe. Though largely self-educated, Walter Pfautsch was an intelligent man and a strong pillar of his community of 6,000. Almost every night after supper he would be involved in some activity. "It got to be the family joke," Lloyd recalled. "Let's see, it's Monday night, Dad must be at church council meeting; Thursday night at church choir rehearsal; Friday night at the Masonic Lodge, where he was secretary for 45 years and a Scottish Rites Templer as well." In midwestern America it was common for men of the middle class to join a lodge. Masons and Oddfellows served the Protestants while the Roman Catholic equivalent was the Knights of Columbus. In addition he found time to be on the board of a local building and loan association. Further he would usually be the first one to call on any friend or acquaintance who was hospitalized. Clearly he provided an admirable role model for his children, not only by what he said to them, but even more effectively by what he did with his life.[5]

All of the Walter Pfautsch family was musical. Walter sang bass and Ouida played the piano. Music-making was a part of family life. Of the children Lloyd was the only one to make it his career, but Marian was a cellist and Walter Jr. also sang in a quartet as he was growing up in Washington. Lloyd's talent first proved to be beyond the ordinary when he was chosen to sing "Away in a Manger" for a Sunday School Christmas pageant when he was at the tender age of three. What he remembered most is that no fear was involved, just the pleasure of successfully performing in public. It was that sense of pleasure that kept him singing for the rest of his youth.

While still in the third grade Pfautsch decided to enter the Franklin County Festival Competition in music. He received second prize. The competition was open to all elementary school students through the eighth grade, so he must have been among the youngest contestants. Encouraged by his success, he entered again in fourth grade and this time placed first. "I remember the piece I sang," he said, "it was 'A Toy Balloon.'" Because the competition rules required that the first place winner retire from future competitions he was no longer able to compete vocally until high school. At the time this did not seem quite fair to him.

But the young Pfautsch continued to sing for the sheer enjoyment of it, joining as many groups as were available to him. And with the strong German background in the town there were abundant opportunities. The more prosperous town fathers saw to it that there were artistic outlets both in the school system and in the town. That a town of 6,000 had its own civic orchestra speaks well of their influence.

Because he kept singing, Lloyd never did really experience a breaking voice in the way many pubescent males do. He just slowly moved down the scale from boy soprano in eighth grade, to first tenor in ninth grade to second tenor as a sophomore and baritone as a junior. By his senior year he finally settled into a bass voice. At the time he was sorry, because his heroes were movie star tenors such as Nelson Eddy. But his top note was only an F above middle C, so he learned to capitalize on his low range instead, easily singing down to low C. This ability later provided his entrée to professional music circles when he arrived in New York. He simply enjoyed singing whenever possible although he had no intention of turning it into a career.

During all four years of high school he competed in what was called the Colony Festival. When interviewed for the SMU campus newspaper decades later he wistfully stated that one thing he would change about his life if he could was that he would have started his music training earlier. "I am a latecomer to music," he told the interviewer. "I really didn't start studying music seriously until three years after college. In my grade school days when my parents made it possible for me to take piano lessons I should have done that more seriously."[6] He continued to harbor that regret even in retirement, feeling that it hampered his abilities in both composing and conducting.

Certainly music was not Lloyd Pfautsch's only interest. He remembered loving to swim in the Missouri River. He also played a lot of softball while growing up. In fact he was a sports enthusiast, writing a sports column for the *Washington Missourian* for most of his high school years. He used the column to argue passionately for his favorite sport, softball.[7] Then, too, his family took somewhat regular trips to St. Louis, thirty miles east of Washington, to see family and (on rare occasions) to take in a performance at the famous Municipal Opera in Forest Park. Like most small-town youth he was allowed to participate in many school-sponsored activities: cultural, intellectual, and athletic. He lettered for three years in basketball. "We weren't a terribly good team, but we had a lot of fun!" He was also on a winning debate team, acted in plays, and participated in student government, serving as vice president of his senior class. He was a representative to the State of Missouri Student Senate for Franklin County, chosen by getting the highest score in his school on a Civics exam. His group was permitted to submit a resolution for a city tax, but it was eventually tabled. He was academically successful as well, being one of four seniors admitted to the National Honor Society and one of seven (out of thirty-eight) listed on the honor roll, for maintaining a grade of "S- (Superior)" or above throughout their public school education.

Meanwhile Pfautsch maintained his strong interest in music during his high school career. He sang in the choir, the men's chorus, and a quartet. He also played tuba in the band and contra-bass viol in the orchestra. Clearly he was drawn to bass instruments, no matter the medium. He claims that tuba and bass viol were chosen because the school owned the instruments and his family did not have to buy them. Further, he notes, he already could read bass clef! Perhaps, but it seems there might be a bit more to it than that.

Although he claimed to play contra-bass viol because it was not very difficult and he could do well without much practice, it is obvious that he was more than a casual performer on this instrument, too. In his junior year, Pfautsch's band, chorus, and orchestra director, Wilfred Crawford, nominated him for membership in the National Youth Orchestra, which was to play in St. Louis. Crawford told him, "I am going to nominate you for this All-Music Educator's National Conference [MENC] Orchestra, but you have to promise me you will practice if you get in!" As one might expect, Pfautsch was as good as his word. He attacked this practice with the discipline and focus with which he undertook any task, particularly a musical one. Crawford provided him with a room off the gymnasium equipped with a record player, so he could listen to 78-rpm recordings of the literature he was to learn and practice with them. He considered Crawford a major influence on his musical life, "encouraging me and challenging me." In an appropriate twist he was able to repay Crawford two decades later by recommending him for the post of chair of the Music Department for the entire Dallas school system. Crawford ended up spending many happy years in Dallas, once again in the same town as one of his prize pupils.

Pfautsch considered the intensive week he spent rehearsing and performing in St. Louis with the National Youth Orchestra to have been a major formative experience in his musical education. He was not only selected for the group, but after an audition in front of the principal bass of the Minneapolis Symphony he was placed fourth chair out of thirteen bass viol players from around the country. This was achieved in spite of the fact that he had only learned the fingerings through second position and just made up fingerings for the rest! He said, with typical modesty, "this taught me two things: (1) I did not know as much as I should and there was still a lot for me to learn. (2) It is not enough just to have a good ear." The whole experience was "tremendously exciting." The conductor was the famous Russian-American violist/conductor Vladimir Bakaleinikov, maestro of the Pittsburgh Symphony. Howard Hanson, director of the Eastman School of Music, was also there to conduct his *Merrymount Suite.* Bakaleinikov conducted Mussorgsky's *Night on Bald Mountain*, the Franck *Symphony in d minor* and Wagner's *Overture to Tannhauser.*[8] Pfautsch was most impressed by the discipline and seriousness of his fellow players and by the beauty of the music chosen. He found it a first-rate orchestra and felt honored to participate. It was exhilarating to be among so many peers who thought of themselves as musicians. As usual he was in awe of them since he only considered his music-making to be an avocation. Although he did not pursue his bass viol playing after high school, the orchestral experience was to prove invaluable later in his professional life, when he was expected to conduct both choral and instrumental ensembles.

Lloyd Pfautsch completed his public school education as a star in arts, athletics, and academics. He was only the second person in the history of the school to earn five bars on his school letter. Points were awarded for sports, clubs, honor roll, and musical organizations and the like. He simply accumulated more than anyone else in his class. In his usually understated manner, he reflected, "I didn't really think anything of it at the time, but later I was grateful that I was allowed to participate so broadly in activities. It was a very sound education for my future." He felt then and still felt late in life that he was "lucky, very lucky" to have spent his childhood and youth in Washington, Missouri.[9]

When it came time to choose a college for their sons, the Pfautsches naturally turned to a nearby prominent institution sponsored by the Evangelical and Reformed Church, Elmhurst College in suburban Chicago. Lloyd had also been accepted to Central College in Missouri and offered a scholarship. But in June, shortly after his high school commencement, a solo quartet from Elmhurst College sang a concert in Washington. Afterwards he talked to the first tenor who encouraged him to choose Elmhurst by saying, "I am sure we can get you a scholarship and besides I know of this small Presbyterian Church in Maywood (Illinois) that needs a choir director, which would earn you some spending money." This and the fact that his older brother had gone to Elmhurst made it the logical choice and in 1939 he matriculated there, pursuing a pre-ministerial course with majors in philosophy, sociology, and religion.

Although Pfautsch had been allowed to conduct the band, orchestra, and chorus from time to time during high school, he claimed, "I was just waving my arms; I did not really know what I was doing." When he took the job in Maywood he admitted that he was far too inexperienced to be effective. He kept the Presbyterian job for three years, but he admitted that he was learning a lot more than the choir members were and that he did not do a very good job. At the end of his junior year the choir president approached him and said, "I am afraid we are going to have to use somebody else next year. You know, Lloyd, I just do not think that conducting is in your future!" While this was a bit devastating to the young musician, the irony is, of course, that conducting *was* Pfautsch's future, as will later become clear.

Fortunately for the world of choral music, Pfautsch was the kind to get up after a fall and get right back onto the horse for another ride! His reaction to being fired from the Presbyterian Church was "I learned to face failure, to be judged and found wanting." Three months later, however, the choir director's job at St. Peter's Evangelical and Reformed Church, the college church in Elmhurst, suddenly became vacant when their director died. Lloyd was invited to take that position. By soliciting the help of many members of the college choir he was able to turn a very small church choir into an impressive group of fifty to sixty intergenerational voices. In fact the choir soon outgrew the front choir stalls and had to take over the balcony. This created distance problems with the organ and organist so he primarily used *a cappella* anthems. Pfautsch viewed this logistical situation as something of a blessing, providing the reason for him to do more *a cappella* music and less that needed accompaniment. He received approbation from both the choir and the congregation and finally was convinced that "I *can* do it, after all!" He also received encouragement at the college, being asked to conduct his own composition for his own Baccalaureate Service. That event marked the first time his parents saw him conduct a choir of the quality of the Elmhurst ensemble.

Lloyd's attitude about music was not much different at Elmhurst College than it had been in high school. It was a pleasant, stimulating avocation, and now a source of income as well. As in high school he also continued to enjoy athletic success, playing on the baseball team all four years. He continued to send information back to the *Washington Missourian* sports writer from time to time. One such article notes that Elmhurst was having a winning season and that Pfautsch, who played third base, was "batting well over 300." But he had also been seduced by the art of choral conducting and for the first

At bat for Elmhurst College Softball team (c. 1941)

three summers after study at Elmhurst College he returned home to Washington and organized the Washington Choral Club "for the fun of singing." Each summer's efforts ended in a public outdoor concert, sharing the program with the Washington Civic Symphony.

Throughout college he studied voice with Ursula Richter. Frau Richter and her husband, Werner, were recent refugees from Nazi Germany. Their escape had been helped by the efforts of renowned theologians Paul Tillich and Reinhold Neibuhr. It was a boon to Elmhurst and to the Richters that they were able to be on that college's faculty. Pfautsch remembered Frau Richter's teaching as a major influence on his interest in singing and on his appreciation of fine vocal repertoire. Lloyd also sang in the mixed chorus and the men's glee club, both directed by Waldimar Hille. It was on tours with these choirs that his legendary interest in playing pool came to light! He enjoyed relaxing with cue in hand, predicting he could put the "ten ball in the corner pocket." Even here his focus and practice habits yielded success. He was often undefeated throughout a tour!

In Pfautsch's junior year at Elmhurst College the Fred Waring Glee Club sponsored a national contest to find the nation's best university men's glee club. The Elmhurst club was chosen, along with seven other choirs, and allowed to compete at New York's Carnegie Hall. The men of the glee club were sent to New York on Pullman cars at Elmhurst's expense. The distinguished panel of judges for the New York finals included Deems Taylor, George Abbott, Richard Bonelli, André Kostelanetz, Wilfred Pelletier, Peter Wilhousky, John Findley Williamson, and Fiorello LaGuardia (presumably an honorary, *ex officio* member!). Pfautsch remembered the excitement at Elmhurst as students gathered to listen to the winners being announced on national radio. When Elmhurst's name was spoken the students burst into spontaneous cheering and applause and a school

Pool Champion at work: Elmhurst College Choir Tour (c. 1942)

dance was improvised on the spot! The impromptu celebration lasted well into the night.

Again, as it had in high school, the opportunity for amateur music-making at a national level provided a pivotal experience in Pfautsch's musical education. He was excited and stimulated by the high quality of musicianship at this contest. More important though, after he sang a solo in Earl Robinson's "Ballad for Americans," a singer/arranger/conductor for the Waring organization, one Robert Shaw, sought him out to congratulate him on the solo, as did the composer. Shaw also worked with the Elmhurst Glee Club during their stay in the Big

Apple. Pfautsch felt that the special interest Shaw paid to his glee club was because it was the only church-related ensemble in the finals of the contest.[10] Shaw's father had been a minister and from time to time Shaw himself considered that calling. Shaw even conducted the group on the steps of City Hall when they sang for the mayor. During rehearsals Lloyd remembered that he removed his shirt and conducted in his undershirt because it was such a warm day and conducting was, for Shaw, an aerobic exercise. The men from Elmhurst College got to know Shaw that week and, of course, got his autograph before leaving town. Although neither knew it at the time, this seemingly tenuous encounter with Robert Shaw was the beginning of a musical and personal relationship that was to be of vital importance to Pfautsch throughout his professional life.

Still another musical event influenced Pfautsch in his junior year at Elmhurst: he was invited to sing a group of songs at the Spring Choir Concert. In attendance was the father of one of the choir's best sopranos, the renowned Chicago voice teacher, Richard D. DeYoung. DeYoung was so impressed with what he heard at this concert that he decided to write a review for the Elmhurst city newspaper. Nearly one quarter of the lengthy review is about Pfautsch's singing. Largely complimentary, DeYoung states, "His greatest gift, however, lies in the field of interpretation. . . . Rarely in student recitals does one encounter a young man or woman with an imagination, and the courage as well as the vocal equipment to use it. . . . This young man could go far in the musical field if he chose to do so."[11]

DeYoung, of course, proved to be more prophetic in his assessment than had the president of the Presbyterian choir in Maywood. Interpretation was always a strength of Pfautsch's choral performances and imagination abounds in his compositions. The predictably understated reaction from Pfautsch to DeYoung's critique was "it certainly didn't hurt my morale."

In his senior year at Elmhurst Pfautsch began his relatively brief career as a voice teacher. He was awarded a scholarship to teach voice to the men in the glee club and to act as assistant conductor. He freely admitted, "I did not really know what I was doing." His only other stints as a voice teacher were several years later at Illinois Wesleyan University and as an interim on the voice faculty at Southern Methodist University. By the time these opportunities arose he did know what he was doing and, in fact, had several successful students.

Keeping up with all of these athletic and musical activities caused Lloyd to have some grades below those he felt he was capable of achieving. He later regretted occasionally placing extracurricular activities first, even though those same activities helped mold him into what he became as a mature adult. Perhaps the tension more accurately lay in the conflict that he faced between the career he was supposed to pursue (theology) and the one he ultimately needed to choose (music). He was in denial of this crucial conflict throughout his undergraduate years at Elmhurst.

Pfautsch graduated from Elmhurst College with a bachelor of arts degree in 1943. He still maintained at this stage that he was seeking a vocation in the ministry and ordination in the Evangelical and Reformed Church, not a career in music. But these tensions never lay very far below the surface through his otherwise halcyon undergraduate years. Pastoral ministry was what he was training for and, more to the point, was what he was expected to do. He admitted that a couple of his pre-ministerial classmates told the girl he was then dating: "He's actually going to end up in music." His response was always "No, I'm not, no, I'm not!" He did, on the other hand, choose to seek his bachelor of divinity degree at Union Theological Seminary partly because of the fame of its Master of Sacred Music program. Few other seminaries of Union's stature offered music degrees. Furthermore, in his senior year he composed a set of *12*

Ex. 1 "Camp Song," 1943 unpublished manuscript

Responses to be sung at a special worship service he was attending. He wisely sought the help of his college choral conductor, Waldimar Hille, in editing the seven-page manuscript. Although it seems a bit puerile when placed next to his later work, it shows, nevertheless, incipient signs of many of his budding writing techniques. For example, his rhythms are derived from the text, he varies the texture by writing SATB, SSA, TBB, solo with SATB background, and the like.[12] Certainly the inclination towards a career in music, if not the intent, was already there. It probably started as early as high school, but now was to the point of festering.

In order to earn money before entering graduate school, Pfautsch went to Detroit for the summer following his Elmhurst graduation. He worked on the line in a steel mill, moving steel doors along a production line. "It was hard work, but it gave me good exercise and paid better wages than I could find in Washington." Summer profits in hand, the eager theology student set off for New York City and a radically different way of life than he had yet experienced.

Chapter 2

The Dance of Promise

(New York City)

IT WOULD BE AN UNDERSTATEMENT to call Pfautsch's decision to go to Union Theological Seminary merely a significant one. His entire life (spiritual, professional, and personal) was forever changed in very positive ways because of his experiences at the seminary and in New York City. What he learned while pursuing two degrees at the famous school, combined with the professional musical opportunities he was afforded in that cultural Mecca, provided highly important, lasting influences upon the young scholar-musician from Washington, Missouri.

When he arrived at Union he professed to be pursuing a bachelor of divinity degree with the eventual purpose of seeking ordination in the Evangelical and Reformed Church, a plan that his parents had mapped out for him at age eighteen, when he left home for his undergraduate experience at Elmhurst College. He was not, he insisted, destined for a career in music. But he experienced almost immediate and sustained success as a professional singer and that encouraged him to reassess his career goals. He also dabbled in composition throughout his years at Union, spending more time and effort on it once his Sacred Music studies began.

Upon arrival in New York Pfautsch auditioned for Clarence and Helen Dickinson. By this time the Dickinsons had retired as directors of the Master of Sacred Music program at Union but remained directors of music at Manhattan's prominent Brick Presbyterian Church and still taught some courses at Union. Pfautsch sang, "Why do the Nations . . ." from Handel's *Messiah* as his audition piece. He asked

Publicity photo used while in New York (1948)

Dr. Dickinson if he could transpose the aria (at sight) down a whole step. The answer was "sure." So Pfautsch sang in the more comfortable lower key and was immediately hired for the Brick Church's all-paid choir. The chance to sing so much important repertoire, including full oratorios each week of Advent and Lent, was both invaluable and pleasurable. He kept this job for all three years of his ministerial studies. He also studied voice throughout those three years. His first elective course at the seminary was Helen Dickinson's History of Church Music. This experience served to increase his interest in the field of sacred music. In the third year he was also employed to conduct the high school choir at the Brick Church. His success in this job helped to foster what became his greatest professional passion: conducting choirs, particularly choirs of youth and young adults. The urge for an education in church music was beginning to gnaw at him.

But Pfautsch took his theological studies seriously. While music-making was both a good source of income and a genuine pleasure, he was still preparing for ordination. After his first year in seminary, he held summer church jobs at two very small, upstate New York parishes (Helena and Bresher Falls). Because of their severe winter weather these towns only held services in the summer months. One of his parishioners loaned him a car, named "Big Bertha," so that he could travel more easily between the parishes. The next two summers were spent at Glen Rock Community Church in New Jersey. He was also involved in student government and was elected president of his senior class at the seminary. A good citizen of the seminary community, he petitioned both Hugh Porter, director of the MSM program, and the president of the seminary for permission to form an ad hoc men's chorus among the seminarians. Both men agreed and Porter even arranged for him to perform Brahms's *Alto Rhapsody* for a UTS chapel service, with Carol Brice singing the solo and Porter him-

Big Bertha – a loaner car to transport Pfautsch and youth groups between Helena and Bresher Falls, NY (1943)

self accompanying. Since this was his senior year, the group ended its brief life with one successful Brahms performance. Pfautsch also composed in his (non-existent) spare time. He completed his "Opus 3," a *Requiem Mass*, while still a theology student. It remains unpublished and was not, to the composer's recollection, ever performed. His use of the label "Opus 3" indicates that he did plan on continuing to compose. He was able to reuse the Sanctus movement for a *Requiem* he wrote on commission in 1981.

Pursuing a pre-theological program at Elmhurst and a bachelor of divinity at Union Theological Seminary caused the Washington, Missouri, draft board to classify Pfautsch as 4D. So the emerging musician was not drafted for service in World War II. But, when the war continued and US involvement deepened, he and one of his Elmhurst classmates who was also in the bachelor of divinity program at Union did apply to the US Navy for appointments to the Chaplaincy. In spite of their 4D status, they were motivated by a patriotic spirit and by the fact that Chaplains-in-Training had their seminary education paid by the US Navy. This was one early example of Pfautsch's penchant for frugality. The two young theologs made

Ex. 2 Requiem Mass, Opus 3 (unpublished, c. 1945)

their way to New York City's Naval Recruitment Center, near Times Square. Even though Lloyd was young, highly intelligent and athletic, he was rejected from service due to blue-green colorblindness. His friend was also rejected, because he was one-half inch too short! So on that day the pursuit of any active duty in the armed forces came to an abrupt halt. The two shared a soda and some ice cream at Bernie's Drug Store (Broadway and 120th) and went back across the street to their studies at Union Theological Seminary.

In 1945 Lloyd Pfautsch's professional singing career reached new heights of success. He studied voice throughout his Union years, first with Maude Neidlinger and then with the English opera star, Clytie Hine Mundy. Still a paid soloist at the Brick Presbyterian Church, he decided to audition for Toscanini's NBC Symphony Chorus. His audition with chorus master Peter J. Wilhousky was memorable for two reasons. It was his first professional audition and he was the very first person to be auditioned. After singing only ten measures or so he was invited to the callbacks and dismissed. The other significant event was that at this audition he first caught sight of alto Edith Herseth, to whom he was immediately attracted. It was truly love at first sight. Fortunately she, too, was invited to the callbacks. Both he and Herseth were successful in the second auditions as well and were among the very few new singers chosen for the chorus. Thus it is true that Arturo Toscanini, albeit unknowingly, brought Lloyd and Edie Pfautsch together, a relationship that lasted fifty-seven years! The Italian maestro's rehearsals provided the opportunity for the relationship to develop, during breaks and before and after rehearsal. Pfautsch also achieved "on-call" status with both the NBC and CBS choruses, singing with many famous conductors during that period.

Pfautsch remembers the work with Toscanini fondly. While the fiery Italian could be very unpleasant to any orchestral player he found lacking, he also had such enormous charisma that "you knew you were going to do your very best; nothing less. It was expected." The legendary conductor also expected it of himself. He could just walk into the room and it made a difference. He conveyed phrasing, dynamics, and other nuances with total clarity and the necessary precision to achieve outstanding ensemble. His rehearsal discipline was absolute—no talking allowed ever! Pfautsch admits that today *Il Maestro* could never get away with his more outrageous behavior, due to unions and to a change in relationship between conductors and players. But he also had those expressive eyes that let the ensemble know what he was feeling. And, somewhat surprisingly, he had a sense of humor. Pfautsch remembers one time when he wanted the chorus to sing more softly and subtly he stopped the chorus and shouted, "Coro, Coro, too loud, too loud! Yes? Yes? More like singing from Brooklyn!" Pfautsch himself used that concept the first time he conducted the *Messiah* in Dallas. They got to "Lift up your Heads" at the end of Part Two and he stopped the chorus and proclaimed "Chorus, chorus, like coming from a distance, like you were singing in Fort Worth!" At the time the choir enjoyed the joke and the effect was achieved. However, several years later he was again conducting that oratorio in Dallas and when they got to the last number in Part Two one tenor raised his hand and said, "Dr. Pfautsch, there is one thing here I do not understand." "Well, what is it?" Pfautsch inquired. The young man replied, "Someone has written in the score 'Fort Worth!'" So the whole story, including the Toscanini connection, was explained to the choir's delight.

Among the other important conductors and composers with whom Pfautsch worked while in New York were Leonard Bernstein, Igor Stravinsky, Paul Hindemith, and Lukas Foss. He only worked with Bernstein once: a spoken part in Marc Blitzstein's *Airborne*

Symphony. They recorded the work and also sang it over NBC. But he sang with Stravinsky several times. He recorded *Symphony of Psalms* twice and also sang it live over CBS radio, all with the composer conducting. He found Stravinsky a "square" conductor, with an unexpressive beat pattern. Pfautsch recalled: "He knew what he wanted and he would usually get it, but not through his conducting technique. He got it through just being there and standing in front of you so you could sort of tell in his eyes what he wanted. When he corrected you he had that nice, deep Russian bass voice." The relationships with Hindemith and Foss were due to his work with Robert Shaw and will be discussed below.

During the theology school years Pfautsch had quite a few professional singing engagements away from New York, as well. He was in great demand for singing the title role in Mendelssohn's *Elijah* and the bass solos in Handel's *Messiah*. He further built a reputation as perhaps the best narrator in the nation for Honegger's *King David.*

One *Messiah* performance at the First Methodist Church of McAllen, Texas, was attended by a standing-room-only crowd of more than 1,000 people. Many had to be turned away when the congregation exceeded the church's capacity.[1] It was conducted by V. Earl Copes, who had been an MSM candidate at Union during Pfautsch's first years of ministerial studies. Pfautsch managed to provide some "cliff-hanger" excitement before the performance. Due to foul weather, his plane from New York was grounded in Winston-Salem, North Carolina, overnight. However, he was finally able to get a plane to Houston, where he was met by a private plane and pilot from Mission, Texas. They arrived in McAllen only two hours before the performance! He had time to dress and get to the performance, but without the benefit of rehearsal with the conductor, the orchestra, or the choir. Nevertheless, the *Basso* sang beautifully and the evening was deemed a huge success. The young New York singer also performed oratorio solos in Lancaster, Pennsylvania; Dallas and Houston, Texas; Patterson, New Jersey; Lindsborg, Kansas; Berea, Ohio; and Lakewood, Ohio, to name a few. But none was accompanied by quite such dramatic circumstances.

In spite of all his oratorio success, however, Pfautsch never attempted to break into the opera world. His own typically modest assessment was that "my voice did not have the requisite amplitude—it was more of an intimate, *lieder* kind of voice. Besides, I knew that I was not a good-looking guy—would not look good on the stage." In spite of all of his vocal accomplishments Pfautsch felt that he would never be at the top of the field as a singer and so he began to cultivate his true love, conducting. Here he clearly did reach the top ranks of his profession.

The year 1946 was full of excitement, productivity, challenge, frustration, and romance. Pfautsch graduated from Union with a bachelor of divinity degree. That spring he had been asked to come to Columbus, Ohio, for an interview at a large Evangelical and Reformed church. The senior pastor, the father of one of his fellow choristers at Elmhurst College, knew of him and his abilities and wanted him to serve as associate pastor and also conduct the choirs. He was interested partly because there were good schools there where he could take the undergraduate work he lacked for admittance to the MSM program at Union. He already had in mind that he wanted to return to Union some day for a second degree. After returning from the Ohio interview he waited several weeks and finally decided to call Columbus. The senior minister was apologetic for not getting back to him, but then told Lloyd that the church had decided to go with a candidate from their own seminary (Eden) in Webster Groves, Missouri. Ironically, Eden was only forty miles from where Pfautsch had grown up and was the seminary his parents preferred that he attend. That church's decision to go with "one of their own" in terms of seminary training was a fairly typical reaction to graduates of Union Seminary. Although Union was widely recognized as the most famous seminary in the United States, it was also considered to be a hotbed of theological liberalism and only the most progressive and socially conscious congregations were likely to seek their clergy from Union. It was a school where socialist ideas were not only tolerated, but at times encouraged. However, this rejection by the Ohio church also provided one more indicator that Pfautsch's choice of Union and New York had changed his life dramatically and forever. This was a defining moment as the young scholar reassessed his options.

Pfautsch was sitting in Bernie's Drug Store, the popular seminary student hangout across Broadway from Union Theological Seminary, when he called the E and R church in Columbus. After learning of his rejection by that church, he hung up the phone in something of a daze. As he sat down, "It was like a sudden conversion, like St. Paul . . . like 'BOING!' I immediately walked across the street to see if I could talk to Hugh Porter, dean of the School of Sacred Music at Union. I walked into his office, sat down and told him I would appreciate it if he would consider me for the MSM program." Porter knew of Pfautsch's professional vocal career and had used him for solos with the seminary choir as well as accompanying him for the previously mentioned Brahms performance. But he replied that Pfautsch would need to make up the undergraduate work, especially theory, that he lacked as a non-music major. He then said, "Of course, we do not have any housing for you this late in the summer." But Pfautsch pointed out that he and Edith Herseth were soon to be married and that her two roommates were also getting married and leaving, so Edith's apartment would work out quite well. Often after that Edie said that

Lloyd only married her because he needed an apartment! Meanwhile private theory lessons were arranged with Adjunct Professor Wallace McPhee, the organist and choirmaster at First Baptist Church of Montclair, New Jersey, and Pfautsch entered the MSM degree on a probationary status as a student "by exception."

A wedding notice from the society page of the *Bertha* (Minnesota) *Herald* for September 7, 1946, reads:

> At three o'clock Saturday afternoon, September 7th, to the strains of Bach's *Air for the G String* Miss Edith Lucille Herseth, daughter of Mr. And Mrs. Adolph A. Herseth, Bertha, Minnesota, met Lloyd Alvin Pfautsch, son of Mr. and Mrs. Walter A. Pfautsch, Washington, Missouri, at the altar of St. Paul's Evangelical Lutheran Church in Bertha. The Reverend Mr. George B. Eschenbacher, pastor of St. Paul's Church, officiated, prompting the vows for the double ring ceremony.

The lengthy article also lists the rest of the music for the ceremony. Miss Elsie Berge, of Minneapolis, played "Jesu, Joy of Man's Desiring" and *Bist Bei Du Mir* by Bach as well as other organ selections. John Herseth, brother of the bride, sang Franck's "O Lord Most Holy" and Beethoven's *Ich Liebe Dich*. The Recessional was Beethoven's *Ode to Joy* ("Joyful, Joyful, We Adore Thee"). The happy couple then returned to New York and Edie's apartment so Lloyd could begin his MSM studies and, soon after that, a family.

Still hoping to meet his parents' expectations for him, Pfautsch also started a student pastorate in 1946. He took a job with the small Edgehill Church in Spuyten Deyvil, in the Bronx. However, starting a new degree and a new life as a married man while maintaining a very active professional singing career did not leave much time or energy for working at the church. Gradually Pfautsch realized

Edie and Lloyd Pfautsch cut the wedding cake whilst both sets of parents look on approvingly. (1946)

that his call was to a music ministry and so the Bronx pastorate was short-lived. Instead he began a job conducting the choir at the First Congregational Church of Manhassatt, Long Island. The position of choirmaster at this upper-middle-class suburban church proved to be much better suited to him than any previous church position he had held, with the possible exception of his senior year in college at the E and R church in Elmhurst. He described Manhassatt as "an almost utopian situation." Most of the choir members had sung in Ivy League glee clubs or choirs, read well, sang well, and expected to take rehearsals seriously. Then, too, the organist was his close friend and classmate, Frank Bohnhorst. Bohnhorst was later to be his colleague at Illinois Wesleyan as well. He started the year in Manhassatt with twenty-eight in the choir and finished it with sixty! Among them were Wall Street lawyers, the head of personnel for Sylvania, an editor of a major publishing house, and the like. Pfautsch remembered, "they just loved rehearsing and they just loved each other. It was a young, burgeoning church at the time and we had to have two services. Many of the choir sang in both services each week." He held that job for the next two years until his MSM degree was finished. The Long Island job was yet another fortuitous event in Pfautsch's career, further defining his destiny.

The Master of Sacred Music degree program at Union was both a challenge and a source of pleasure. Pfautsch felt inferior to many of his classmates, at least in terms of preparation. They came from demanding undergraduate music majors at schools such as The Eastman School and The Curtis Institute while he had only studied voice and one course in music history at Elmhurst. He was especially challenged by theory classes. A course in Aural Harmony, in which the emotional qualities of chords were analyzed, was nearly his undoing. "My grade in there was a pure gift!" On the other hand, Pfautsch had many things going for him: he was slightly older and more mature than most of his classmates, he had far more professional music experience at the highest levels, he was married and consequently better focused than many, and he had already passed all the required theology courses with very high marks. It was not surprising to anyone except Pfautsch that he received the scholarship awarded to the second year student with the highest grade point average for his first year studies. To him it was both amazing and a real morale booster. He had once again proven that talent and hard work are a formidable combination. He also proved that Hugh Porter made the right decision in admitting him by exception to the MSM program.

When Pfautsch began his MSM degree, conducting was taught

at Union Theological Seminary by four faculty: Lowell Beveridge (Columbia University faculty), Alfred Greenfield (associate professor at New York University and chair of the Music Department for NYU's University College), Morris Wynn Watkins (director of the University Women's Chorus of New York) and David McK. Williams (director-emeritus of St. Bartholomew's Church.)[2] Students were to study with each of the four. Pfautsch felt that Greenfield was "head and shoulders above the rest as a teacher, as a model and as a person." He always believed that among the faculty at Union, Greenfield and Harold Friedell, his composition teacher, were the strongest influences upon his musical growth. He admired both teachers because they were able to teach, to criticize, and to challenge their students without ever putting them down by making caustic or humiliating comments. Of Friedell he said, "I never felt under Friedell that anybody in the class was intimidated or discouraged from saying what they felt about someone else's composition. You always got positive feedback before you got negative feedback. He always balanced the two." He noted that his own supportive, encouraging style of teaching owed a debt to the models provided by Greenfield and Friedell.

Pfautsch felt so strongly about the lack of good teaching from the other conducting faculty, though, that he organized his classmates and together they asked Dean Hugh Porter to call a meeting with the conducting faculty to discuss their concerns. Porter had had enough complaints that he did this and Pfautsch served as the main spokesperson for the students. Trying to use the same positive approach that he himself had responded to so well under Greenfield and Friedell, he began, "I know that the intention of each of the faculty is to share their experience with us and help us then gain experience with conducting techniques. But I, for one, feel that the teaching is not done in a sequential way. We get up, we are told to be ready to conduct such and such a piece. We conduct and then we are criticized for not doing what was expected of us to do, but we did not know what was expected of us to do! We have no preparation for working with those pieces. I feel we need to go through fundamentals in a sequential way so that we are able then to practice and prepare for what we have to do." Pfautsch also made the case for adding an anthem repertoire class for all MSMs. Pfautsch felt that it was a good session and that he and the other students had been heard. He was right in that the next year David McK. Williams was replaced by Leon Barzun. Like Greenfield, Barzun was an orchestral conductor in the New York area and shared his belief in teaching beat patterns, beat pattern control, facility within the patterns, and the like. "It changed the conducting classes completely and we were all much happier."

Not all of his conducting experiences in the second year were happy ones, though. Alfred Greenfield had organized a series of concerts in which all of the MSM students were expected to conduct. The singers and organists for the concert were their own classmates. Lloyd was assigned to conduct the fiendishly fast "Then did Elijah break forth" from Mendelssohn's *Elijah*. His accompanist, who shall remain nameless, was from Texas and considered the best organist in the class. For some reason pride got the better of him and he announced to Pfautsch just before the performance that he was going to play the accompaniment from memory! The young conductor replied, "I'm not happy about that, it's a difficult accompaniment and hard for the choir to sing." But the recalcitrant organist did it anyway. Predictably, on the top of the second page, as the texture changed, the organ dropped out. A slapping of pages followed as an alert tenor near the console realized the problem and took his score to the organ, opened it and held it in place for the organist. The organist rejoined the choir on the next page. Pfautsch meanwhile gave the choir what he called "the evil eye" in as much as to say "Don't you DARE stop singing!" And they didn't. Afterwards, the foolish organist did apologize, to which Pfautsch replied, "the audience knows who was the problem tonight." Although capable of both tact and grace, the emerging conductor was not always able to apply either under performance pressure.

Harold Friedell was not only a fine teacher for Pfautsch, but he also composed music that the student very much admired. Further, Friedell was very generous in offering to perform his protégé's compositions. He invited Lloyd to sing some of his own solo compositions for an Evensong at St. Bartholomew's, including his solo cantata, *The Faith of Abraham*. At that time this church was the premiere venue for church music in the entire city. Pfautsch considered this "a real shot in the arm" and proof of his mentor's regard for his compositional efforts.

Friedell twice assigned composition projects that turned into published works for the young composer. One of them, *Puer nobis,* was written to fulfill a fall 1947 semester class assignment to compose a Christmas carol. It was not published, however, until 1953, when it became his third work in print. The original version already demonstrates his growing skill with the use of word-oriented rhythms and the subtle changes possible in a very basic accompaniment in order to color or comment on the text. A comparison of the original class assignment completed in October of 1947 with the published version of 1953, however, clearly illustrates his growth from a student to a professional composer with an expanded understanding of the choral sound and how to best write for it. In the original the final verse, "Omega and Alpha He," retains the unison chorus and Spartan choral accompaniment of the previous verses, with only a bit of new figuration for the keyboard part. In the later version, Pfautsch added a counter melody for the oboe and/or flute stops of the organ above the original accompaniment of the interlude before the last verse, now assigned to the left hand and pedal. He also added more figuration to the keyboard writing. When the voices enter again he gave them a two-part canon (TB vs SA) and then retained the original tune in the TB unison voices while the women branch out into

Ex. 3 Puer Nobis, 15 October 1947

two parts for SA. Finally the men receive two parts for TB and he finished the work with true SATB writing, ending with the final two measures of the original accompaniment for the keyboard part, but with the flute/oboe-stop tune superimposed above it. Because he introduced the changes so gradually and subtly, the piece does not sound like an early work with a new verse tacked on. Rather, it moves logically to the new, more complex ending in a very convincing and disarming manner. As will be seen in future compositions, both intelligence of approach and sensitivity of musical expression remained hallmarks of this talented composer's repertoire.

The cantata *Israel at the Red Sea* was his final composition project at Union. Friedell liked it so much that he showed it to Hugh Porter and the two agreed it should be performed in James Chapel for a morning chapel service. Pfautsch remembered that both Robert Shaw and Alice Parker came to the dress rehearsal for the work, to show support and to watch him conduct his own composition. Unfortunately the New York publishers did not immediately share Friedell and Porter's enthusiasm. It, too, was eventually published, but not for forty-three years![3]

Of all the fortuitous circumstances that engulfed Pfautsch when he came to New York City, at the very top of the list was the opportunity to develop a relationship with Robert Shaw. One night soon after he started his studies at Union Seminary, Pfautsch was listening to the radio and happened to catch the Collegiate Chorale's performance of Brahms's Psalm 51, "*Schafe im mir, Gott.*" Like most collegiate choristers, he had sung the motet at Elmhurst and really loved Shaw's performance of it. So he sat down and wrote a fan letter to Shaw, explaining that he had met him when the Elmhurst Glee Club sang in the national competition in New York and just wanted him to know how much he appreciated the fine performance by the

Ex. 4, Israel at the Red Sea, c. 1946

Collegiate Chorale. Soon after that, the fourth floor telephone in Hastings Hall at Union rang. In those days the Union dorms had only one phone per floor and whoever happened to be near it when it rang was expected to answer and then find the person being called.

It was not a perfect system, but this time, thankfully it worked. Lloyd was called to the phone by a star-struck classmate who rather tenuously said, "Err, Robert Shaw wants to talk to you!" Lloyd excitedly picked up the receiver and heard his hero say, "Hello! I got your note and was very glad to hear from you." Pfautsch explained that he was studying at Union and again complimented him on the recorded concert on the radio. "Well, I have a group, the Collegiate Chorale that I rehearse every Monday night. If you are able, please feel free to come and sit in on the rehearsals. By all means, stop by." So Pfautsch, who had basketball practice with a church group in Greenwich Village on Monday nights, found that he could easily get to the chorale practices after basketball finished (about 8 or 8:30 p.m.). He remembered the fun of singing along with the group and then going out for a sandwich and coffee afterward and the chance to chat with the master of the choral art.

Soon after that, Shaw started teaching part-time at The Juilliard School, which in those days was directly across 121st Street from Union Seminary. In one of their post-rehearsal chats Shaw said to Lloyd, "Why don't you come over sometime, if you have time. Drop over if you can. Be happy to have you come around the studio." Finally one day he decided to do just that and gathering his courage, found his way to Shaw's Juilliard studio and knocked on the door. "Come in!" was the reply. As he opened the door he found Shaw hovering over the piano and seated at the keyboard was the noted composer-conductor, Lukas Foss.[4] "Come on in and join us, we're reading through Bach cantatas," came the friendly invitation. Pfautsch had always found reading Bach "like shooting ducks in a barrel," so he did not hesitate to join in. After an hour or so Foss had to leave. Afterwards Shaw said to him, "You know, I'm doing some recordings next month. Would you like to do some recording with me, be in the group?" The eager reply was, "Well, I certainly would!" Shaw continued, "I'll have Billy Johnson call you and see if you can make all the rehearsals and the recording sessions." And that was his audition for Robert Shaw. He was instantly a member of the RCA Victor (later, Robert Shaw) Chorale.[5]

Doing the recordings paid $10 per side of a 78-rpm disc. In 1947 that was a significant sum, especially since the Pfautsches' first baby, Deborah, was born that summer at New York City's Presbyterian Hospital. The group recorded Shaw's first Christmas carol album, Bach's Cantata 4: *Christ lag in todesbonden* and his *Magnificat* as well as Sigmund Romberg favorites, favorite opera choruses and the *Liebeslieder Waltze* of Brahms. He remembered that in the recording sessions they were treated like members of the musicians' union, everything on a strict schedule. But at rehearsals it was more like a volunteer choir, in that rehearsals continued until the maestro was satisfied. But, he noted:

> We really didn't care, because we were all young, we just all did it for the sheer enjoyment. We enjoyed singing as a group and we enjoyed working with Bob in his youthful stage as a conductor, full of energy and vitality. The *esprit* that he developed with the group was just wonderful. We enjoyed each other as people, we respected each other as singers—it wasn't work, it was fun! We were having a delightful time making music with Bob guiding or directing us. He made you feel like everyone was his friend. You could talk to him and he would talk to you.

Later on, Pfautsch discovered, rehearsals became more professional and ultimately it was strictly professional on tour. "I had former students in the touring choirs and their experience was much different from mine. But at this stage we acted like a group of people who loved choral music and Bob was our ringleader."

Pfautsch had particularly fond memories of recording the first Christmas carol album with Shaw. He said, "Whereas our album sounded like a recording of a group that enjoyed singing these carols, the second album, made much later, sounds like a professional chorus hired to sing the music." The earlier group did enjoy singing the carols and that is what comes across, even though they were all professionals, too. "There was a feeling of spontaneity on the first Christmas album that really hits people 'between the ears' when they listen to it!" It was not only one of the first carol albums, it is still one of the most popular. The brass players are first-rate and the arrangements are gorgeous. It may well remain one of the best Christmas albums of all time.

Membership in the chorale varied with the project at hand:

> It would never be exactly the same number of us each time. He would have whatever number he thought was required for that particular piece. Like, there would be more for the *Magnificat* but fewer for the Christmas carols. For the *Liebeslieder Waltzer* there were only 12 of us. There was a nucleus he would keep and then he would add more singers in relation to the demands of a particular recording. For the Bach *B Minor Mass* it was a larger group and RCA decided to pay each of us $100 and two free albums. We felt lucky to get it. However, after all of those very lengthy rehearsals and two performances at Hunter College and the recording sessions, the last of which finally ended at 2:30 a.m., I never wanted to hear or sing the *B Minor Mass* again!

Pfautsch was also privileged to sing on the recording Shaw made of the premiere performance of Paul Hindemith's *When Lilacs Last in the Dooryard Bloom'd; An American Requiem after Walt Whitman.* The recording was made with the composer present and so Pfautsch got to meet the famous German musician and hear his ideas on this exciting and challenging new piece of music. Among other famous members of that initial Victor Chorale were mezzo-soprano Grace Hoffman, singer and conductor Clayton Krehbiel, and singer and choral contractor Tommy Pyle (whose wife was Alice Parker).

Lloyd Pfautsch was never an advocate of choirs singing in quartets or in "salt and pepper" placement. Robert Shaw did use this plan with his chorale but only because on radio broadcasts and recordings with a small group in a studio he could achieve better balance that way. He could put his heaviest and also his most penetrating voices to the back and the lighter, more neutral voices to the front and avoid either having one voice dominate or getting blocks of sound from one section dominating the others. For most university and church choirs Pfautsch regarded quartet placement as a good rehearsal technique, when time permits, but not usually a good performance plan.

When Pfautsch started recording with the chorale, he felt Shaw was a demon about diction. It was essential for the recordings and the radio shows that the words be understood, but Shaw's convictions about the crucial need for clear diction had started much earlier. Fred Waring first heard Shaw when the younger man was conducting the Pomona College Glee Club and was amazed at what he heard Shaw achieve with undergraduates. Waring himself did a lot to improve choral diction for American choirs by including phonetic spellings and syllabification in his hundreds of very popular published choral arrangements. Some of these, incidentally, had been arranged by Shaw.

Through his teaching at Juilliard, Shaw met Madeline Marshall, who also strongly influenced his ideas about diction. She coached and taught diction at both Juilliard and Union Theological Seminary for many years. This writer can attest from personal experience that she was a wise and delightful teacher of a potentially boring subject. Her harsh voice with the strong accent of a Brooklyn Jewess kept classes lively and everyone in focus. Pfautsch, too, was very grateful for her coaching when he narrated *King David* with the Juilliard Chorus and Orchestra. When they finished the Honegger project she gave him a manuscript copy of her forthcoming book. Pfautsch took that with him to Illinois and used it there in conducting classes. Of course, Marshall was originally more concerned with spoken diction than sung diction and Pfautsch, although a fan, did not always agree with the application of her ideas to singing. Eventually he responded by writing his own diction book, but at this stage he used hers. Fortunately it appeared in print the first year he taught in Illinois.

Another important influence on Shaw, who also influenced Pfautsch, was the renowned musicologist Julius Herford. In fact he influenced most of the important choral conductors of his era.[6] Herford was in New York at this time but later taught at Westminster Choir College and then enjoyed a long tenure at Indiana University. Pfautsch remembered that Shaw used to rehearse until 9:30 or 10:00 p.m. at Liederkranz Hall and then catch a cab to go work with Herford into the wee hours of the morning. He had the physical and mental stamina to do it and was determined to learn all that he felt he needed to learn. "Julius was a very good teacher for him," Pfautsch asserted. Aside from absorbing what Shaw learned as it was shared with the chorus in rehearsal, Pfautsch also worked directly with Herford as he was preparing to enter the MSM program at Union Theological Seminary. He clearly understood the concept of analyzing the music one intends to conduct before ever approaching the ensemble for a first rehearsal. As we shall see later, Pfautsch was able to invite Herford to SMU as well, for further study and reflection.

In these early years Robert Shaw was a demon for perfection in matters beyond diction as well. He would get quite irritated when he was not getting the sound he wanted, especially from his professional singers. Pfautsch remembered in the summer of 1947 when the chorale was having trouble with some passage and Shaw got so angry that he started having individual singers stand up and sing. He called on Pfautsch, tenor Clayton Krehbiel, and a soprano and an alto to sing the passage in front of everyone. As it turned out they all could and so the conductor's response was "Now that's the way I want it sung!" Pfautsch admitted that when he moved to Illinois Wesleyan he tried this approach once or twice but found that it could be psychologically damaging to both the selected singers and the rest of the choir. He soon quit this tactic and grew to think of it as abusive to the choir. Most successful conductors today would agree with Pfautsch's final assessment.

But Pfautsch would be the first to admit that most of Shaw's choral techniques had a great and lasting influence on his own conducting style. As Carlton Young observed: "Pfautsch has Shaw's demeanor: if you will just stand in front of me and watch we can make music together. Shaw got this from Fred Waring."[7] "At first," Pfautsch noted, "I was a typical Shaw disciple. I used a lot of his rehearsal procedures. But I had also learned the dangers of blindly copying someone else's style and techniques." Shaw said to him, "You know, I am teaching this conducting class at Juilliard and since you are just across the street if you would like to sit in on it at any time, come on over." So he did attend when he could. The first six weeks consisted of Shaw and Julius Herford talking about the analysis of a Bach motet. Finally the students in class got together and told Robert they really wanted to conduct, that they appreciated the analysis but they really wanted to conduct for his comments and help. So Shaw acquiesced and told them that next time they should be prepared to conduct such-and-such passage from a particular motet. Shaw, Herford, and Pfautsch sat in a horseshoe formation behind the class and observed the students. The first person got up and looked like an imitation of Shaw; his gestures were Shaw's and he bounced around like the maestro. But Shaw, who was nervously rocking back and forth in his chair, turned to Herford and said, "I can't take it anymore, Julius!" Shaw got up and said, "No, you are not doing it right. Let me show you and point out some things to you." He then took over and in his own manner talked to the group while rehearsing and walked around the group and of course things fell into place rather quickly. He turned to the student and said, "You see what I mean?" "Well, yeah, I think so," came the reply. "Well, then try again," the student was directed. So he tried it again and did the same imitation he had done before. And Pfautsch thought to himself "Aha! You can not do it by imitation. You have to know why your mentor did what he did. You can't just look at what he did, you have to analyze what he did and why he did it and then make it your own." The mentor should tell you "I am doing this, making a certain gesture, in order to get this result." "And that," Pfautsch maintained, "is something I started demanding early on in my teaching of conducting. I told my students that I wanted them to know what I did and why, but not merely become puppets of my style. If you have any questions I will try to answer them for you," he would tell them.

In terms of pacing rehearsals, Pfautsch also learned from Shaw. He learned the importance of keeping the momentum going. He also learned not to talk too much. He learned to explain his gestures if they were not clear. For example, Shaw told the Collegiate Chorale "Now look, you should not have any trouble with that *hemiola*. If you just watch I will help you." So Pfautsch added to his growing repertoire of gestures the ability to imitate the *hemiola*, remaining in two but adjusting the rebound to reflect the rhythmic impact of the *hemiola.* Beyond that, but related to it, Pfautsch also learned a lot of tricks for achieving good diction and proper vocal placement by observing and singing with Shaw for those years he was in New York. Again, he learned that he had to apply them to his own situation and to what his ears heard emanating from his choirs. He was then able to assimilate them and adapt them to his own needs.

Another person who strongly influenced Robert Shaw and also had a musical relationship with Pfautsch was Alice Parker. Although she is now widely recognized in her own right as a major composer of American choral music, Parker initially came to public notice as the arranger for most of Robert Shaw's published choral music. She enrolled at Juilliard for the graduate program in conducting under Shaw.[8] She always felt that she was accepted as their token female in the class. Classmates and the instructor denied that. But Shaw soon learned that she was a genius at choral arranging and extremely facile. She began by doing sketches of choral arrangements for Shaw to edit. "If he had something like that he could edit wonderfully," Parker said. "It was just fascinating to watch what he did. He took the most minute details, like where was the consonant going to come? Was it on the first half of the beat or on the last half of the beat. And he examined all the little accompaniment patterns so that they had a life of their own." She noted that a composer could repeat at most three times and then the idea had to go somewhere. "He had such enormous respect for the individual singer that each line had to go somewhere. It was the most incredible schooling!" These arrangements, often timed to be published as the same pieces were released on 78-rpm albums, were at first issued under the Shaw-Parker aegis.

Later, as Shaw had less and less to do with them, they were released as "arranged by Alice Parker."

Parker came to the Collegiate Chorale through a side door. She was married to Tommy Pyle, one of the early members of the chorale and soon a successful choral contractor for Shaw and other professional New York ensembles. Fresh out of undergraduate school, Parker began attending rehearsals with her husband. She still laughs about her audition for the Collegiate Choral. She had no vocal training when she came to New York, but did have an outstanding ear for choral sounds and was blessed with phenomenal pitch accuracy. She was one of only two singers in the history of the chorale to pass the sight-singing exam with no mistakes. But she could not pass the singing exam, as the committee wanted a mature vocal quality that she had not been trained to produce. So she went to Shaw and asked permission to just sit in on the rehearsals, which to her were "like heaven, the air was electric. Shaw was so into it that he made everyone else be into it as well." Shaw said to her, "You mean you didn't pass the audition?" and she replied "No, I don't sing that well." He thought a moment and said, "Well, we worked very hard to get the Chorale set up so that they have their own committees and I can't really contravene their decision. But let me see what I can do. I do hear the voices of those who audition for the small chorus so why don't we schedule you for that audition." So Parker bravely entered the small audition studio where Shaw and his longtime sidekick, Clayton Krehbiel, were ready to listen and Billy Johnson was accompanying at the piano. "I said I would sing Beethoven's *Ich liebe dich*. As I struggled on I could see Billy Johnson's shoulders begin to shake with laughter and Shaw's head was sinking lower and lower until it reached his knees. I kept going through the whole song. When I finished there was dead silence. Then, finally, he looked up and said 'Fantastic . . .

intonation!' He said I could join the choir if I promised to sit in the back row where he would never again have to hear me!" But that also meant that Parker could keep the whole section on pitch. She usually knew exactly what Shaw was going for when he repeated a section, what he was trying to get and she could help in that way. He ever after teased her about her singing, but she survived it, as they formed one of the most successful choral arranging teams of all time. Shaw recognized in Parker, as he had in Pfautsch, an enormous talent that he could use to their mutual benefit and musical growth.

Parker points out that when she first met Lloyd Pfautsch he was very much in the inner circle with Shaw and someone she regarded with awe. She was new and young and on the outside looking in, while he was in the select group for run-out concerts from New York and for almost all of the recordings Shaw made. That same image of Pfautsch as one already acknowledged to be a master musician was seen when he sat with Herford and Shaw behind the conducting class at Juilliard, where he could observe and comment. Parker looks back on those early years in New York as "halcyon days, full of excitement." She fondly recalls that "Lloyd was always both someone who commanded so much respect and affection and who has just stood for wonderful principles in his life and his music and composing. And he has had such a huge impact on so many generations of young people."

Like Pfautsch, Parker considers her music to be *logocentric*. She begins the composing process with a study of the words and then expresses them through music, not the other way around. Pfautsch espoused the same approach. Further, both evaluate new choral music by first examining the text, next the validity of the relationship between the melody and the text, and finally the form and texture and their ability to express that text. Consequently, both absorbed Shaw's famous emphasis on diction and added to his approach their own tricks and techniques to achieve absolute textual clarity with a choir in a way that enhances the meaning of the words and yet sounds completely natural to the listener.

While both Parker and Pfautsch first gained reputations as outstanding arrangers of choral music, they differed in their attitudes about that label. Parker sees no difference between arranging and composing. She points out that the first movement of Bach's *B Minor Mass* is really a choral arrangement of a chorale tune. The same is true for most other chorale or chant-based music and yet no one argues against calling Bach a composer. Pfautsch, on the other hand, shied away from calling himself a composer. He felt that he was a conductor who wrote arrangements for his choir when he needed them. Even though much of his music is based on original composition, rather than settings of existing ones, only late in life did he acknowledge that perhaps he could be considered a composer as well as an arranger and a conductor. He used to feel that one had to make a living by composing in order to assume that mantel. But his publisher and friends often pointed out to him that very, very few composers have not also taught, conducted, and/or performed to round out their careers and pay the bills. Parker, too, as her composing skills matured, concentrated on more original music and less arranged music and is now widely recognized as an important American composer (see end note 6, this chapter). But she has always thought of herself as a composer and so that has been no adjustment for her. It is only in more recent times that she has also gained recognition as a conductor. In that sense her career has been a mirror reflection of Pfautsch's.

In 1948 Lloyd Pfautsch again graduated from Union Theological Seminary, this time with the Master of Sacred Music degree. He was again at a crossroads. He could stay in New York. Robert Shaw had already invited him to join the Robert Shaw Chorale, which was to go on an extensive tour in the fall. Further, his church in Manhassatt was very anxious to keep him as their minister of music and offered to match or exceed any other salary offers he might receive. But the choral bug had finally and completely taken over and there was no doubt in Pfautsch's mind that he wanted a full-time conducting position with a college or university, preferably a church-related one. So Pfautsch applied to the Lutton agency in Chicago, the normal channel in those days for a new teacher seeking an academic position in music. He was in the running for two choral posts at Illinois universities: Illinois Wesleyan and James Millican. As luck would have it his New York choir sang special music for the dedication of their new church in Manhassatt. After the service one of his tenors said, "I would like you to meet my mother." So the two began talking and she said, "I understand you have been looking for a teaching job. Where have you looked?" Pfautsch mentioned the two Illinois schools and the lady exclaimed, "Illinois Wesleyan! Why Merrill Holmes, the president there, is one of my old, dear friends. He and I have been on a lot of Methodist committees together. I believe I will just give him a call." Lloyd dismissed her comment as kind and generous but unlikely to materialize in any significant way. Soon after that he received a telegram from K. C. Lutton saying that he thought Pfautsch was to be offered the James Millican position. That very afternoon he also received a conference call from the president and the dean at Illinois Wesleyan. They offered him their position but wanted an answer that very day. He agreed to accept their offer. The next day, however, James Millican sent a telegram offering him their position at $100 more in annual salary. The Manhassatt Church offered him double the Illinois Wesleyan salary, but he had at last resolutely decided on his career path and packed his bags for Bloomington, Illinois. Although he was by nature extremely frugal, this was one decision that Pfautsch did not make based on financial concerns.

Soon after he arrived in Bloomington, the president and his wife sponsored an afternoon tea for new faculty. The president sat down next to Pfautsch and began chatting. Eventually he said, "You know it's really interesting how I happened to call you when I did. Just the day before that the dean and I had still not made up our minds. But then I received a call from an old friend of mine, who said she had met you at the dedication of her son's Congregational Church in Long Island. She had such nice things to say about you that I just picked up the phone and called the dean and said, 'you know, I think we ought to go after this young man Pfautsch.'" Although he had strong recommendations from Robert Shaw, Hugh Porter, and Robert Baker, it was that call between old friends that actually got the job for the newly minted Union graduate. New York and Union Seminary had yielded a largely happy experience and made an indelible impression upon him, personally and professionally. But now Pfautsch eagerly anticipated his new life and a return to the Midwestern milieu.

Chapter 3

The Dance of Announcement

(Illinois)

It is often true that jobs offered and opportunities presented are fortuitous. Certainly Lloyd Pfautsch felt called to the position at Illinois Wesleyan, but even he could not know what a great match was in the making when he agreed to move to Bloomington, Illinois. He found himself surrounded by colleagues he could respect, students who challenged him to do his best, and an academic life that allowed him time to grow and develop as both a conductor and a composer. He used his decade in Illinois to build his reputation in both fields, becoming nationally recognized in each by the time he was ready to move on. He also had his only opportunity to regularly teach voice at the university level. By the time he finished his work in Illinois he was approaching iconic status among choral musicians in the United States.

Once Lloyd Pfautsch had accepted the new job, the dean at Illinois Wesleyan asked him to move out from New York as soon as possible so that he could begin teaching that first summer. While Edie (and baby Deborah) took this chance to visit Edie's parents in Minnesota, Lloyd went on to Bloomington by himself. He stayed in a room provided by the university that was near the campus. It must have been lonely those first few weeks, although there was plenty to be done. Unlike Manhassatt, all did not seem utopian when he arrived. "There were times as we struggled financially those first couple of years," he admits, "when I wondered if we had made a mistake not staying at Manhassatt" (for nearly twice the salary). He was shocked that the university's choral library was so small that it would fit into one part of the small closet in his studio. A further surprise was that it had never been catalogued. Since he was alone, with nights to himself, he set about cataloguing the choral collection almost as soon as he arrived. It was filled with Fred Waring arrangements, not what he had in mind for the collegiate choir at a quality university. But at least he got it all organized, which satisfied his Germanic need for order.

A few weeks later, his family intact, he was able to move into his house on the campus. It was only two hundred feet or so from the front door of his new abode to his office in Presser Hall, home of the Music Department. This feeling of connectedness and close proximity of venues was one aspect of Bloomington that he found superior to New York. He certainly missed his friends in New York, both at the church and in the city's choral circles, but he had a sense that this was where he should be. To supplement his university salary and continue his relationship with the church, he accepted the job of choirmaster at Second Presbyterian Church of Bloomington. The large, active church required his presence at least three afternoons a week. The main choir there was a youth choir of about seventy-five voices. They were expected to memorize every anthem. After two years he agreed with the church that they needed to return to a full-time minister of music. By then conducting, teaching, and composing were more than enough to keep him busy. At IWU he had started a women's chorus, a men's chorus, and a training choir known as the Chapel Choir as well as conducting his select Collegiate Choir and the amalgam known as the Choral Union.

When he began in the fall of 1948, Professor Pfautsch wanted the Collegiate Choir at IWU to know that he expected to challenge them beyond their previous experiences. He began by starting work on the Bach *Magnificat* for his first Christmas concert with the ensemble. The students soon realized that there was a new conductor on campus! He quickly built a reputation as something of a tyrant in rehearsals.[1] No doubt this was a carryover from his experiences with Robert Shaw and others. He later acknowledged that he found that he could not use Shaw's approach in many instances, since he was not working with a professional ensemble. Gradually he learned what to use, what to adapt, and what to discard. One example is the time the students were getting a bit apathetic in the week before their Christmas concert, feeling like they already knew the music well. So Pfautsch stopped after a few minutes of rehearsal and reseated the groups, mixing up sections as much as possible. That done, he observed, they really took notice and rededicated themselves to the music. When one chorister asked after rehearsal "are we going to sing in this formation again tomorrow?" He replied, "I don't know, come to class tomorrow and see!" In fact he never expected to perform with that seating plan; he merely wanted to regain their musical attention for that particular rehearsal.

As one might expect, it took the students a while to understand and appreciate their new mentor. However, through making choral rehearsals into exciting learning experiences, through his successful voice studio teaching. and through the outstanding artistry of his own vocal recitals he soon gained both the respect and the admiration of his students and colleagues. The choirs found that they could sing challenging music and do it well and still receive the approval of the audiences and congregations who heard them, both on campus and on tour. But this mutual acceptance was not achieved easily or instantly. Attitudes changed slowly and both sides had much to learn. In one of the early years Pfautsch remembers buying the Hindemith *Six Chansons* for the group, planning to sing it on tour that spring. While these lovely *a cappella* pieces are standard literature today and sung by many good high school choirs as well, such was not the case in the late 1940s and early '50s. A couple of the students were so put off by what they considered "Hindemith's modern style" (even though the pieces had been published in 1939!) that they pleaded with Pfautsch not to try and sing them on tour. "People will walk out on us if we try to sing Hindemith on tour." But Pfautsch held his ground and tried to get them to adopt a wait and see attitude. Fortunately the first audience on tour did like the songs and no one walked out on them. In fact, during the intermission of a matinee concert Pfautsch overheard someone in the narthex calling a friend on the phone to say, "You better get over here for the evening concert. I'm going to come back for it. Wait until you hear them sing the Hindemith, they are fabulous!" Naturally, Pfautsch lost no time in relaying the eavesdropped message to his singers. Gradually the choristers began to feel a sense of pride in having sung challenging music well and lost their fear of negative audience responses. Both sides had grown from the experience. Pfautsch remembered, "I knew the students really were glad to have more challenging repertoire. But I was smart enough to give them some of the other stuff (Fred Waring arrangements) as well." From this tenuous, albeit successful, beginning his reputation as a choral conductor grew rapidly. In both 1951 and 1959 he was invited back to his alma mater, Union Theological Seminary, as director of choral activities for their summer session.

In his private voice teaching Pfautsch was a success from the start. His studio was filled with admiring students and his singing career continued on a national basis. "He was a very good voice teacher and I admired him so much for his artistry as a soloist," said renowned concert organist, Robert Anderson, of his student days at Illinois Wesleyan. Anderson, who began his freshman year in 1951, recalls, "He was *the one* to hire if you wanted a narrator for *King David*, he did that a lot. He was also a well-known oratorio singer." In fact Pfautsch sang the title role in Mendelssohn's *Elijah* and the bass solos from Handel's *Messiah* many times during his Illinois years. "Besides that the Collegiate Choir was a very fine group." Anderson not only accompanied the Collegiate Choir, but also sang solos with them. Then, too, his sister Dorothy was a voice student of Pfautsch's, so he was in a position to know a good deal about the conductor-singer-composer and his teaching.[2] Decades later, after their respective retirements from Southern Methodist University as long-term colleagues, each still greatly admired the other.

Pfautsch regarded the years that Robert Anderson was a student at Wesleyan (1951–55) as extremely fulfilling ones. "I had about 10 students of the caliber of Bob Anderson in the choir. Can you imagine 10 Bob Andersons running around your campus? One was a flutist, one a violinist; several were singers or pianists—a really good mix. At least six of them had perfect pitch. So I could do quite demanding works with the choir and still count on them to remain in tune." One example is Aaron Copland's challenging *a cappella* work *In the Beginning*, which was still a new piece at the time (it was published in 1947). Pfautsch regarded the 1954–55 class as the strongest undergraduate group he ever taught.

One member of this high-talent group was Janet Frank, one of Pfautsch's best voice students. Anderson recalls Frank as Pfautsch's favorite student during their years as classmates at Illinois Wesleyan. She went on to Union Seminary with Anderson and served as Ivor Jones' assistant in the choral program. She later sang for several years with the Robert Shaw Chorale, including on their European tours. Frank, now deceased, also taught a lot of Asian students in the New York area and published a book in Japan, on how to learn to sing American pop music, focusing on English diction for Japanese singers. She served as one shining example of Pfautsch's influence as a teacher.

Anderson was not alone in his enthusiastic appraisal of the IWU Collegiate Choir. Pfautsch's Collegiate Choir concerts were beginning to receive favorable national coverage in the musical press. For example, one appearance at Kimball Hall in Chicago elicited these comments: "The conductor and his group achieved excellent results in matters of balance, ensemble and phrasing. The program was selected with impeccable taste and imagination." Also, "the choir reflected the meticulous training and fine taste of its gifted director, Lloyd Pfautsch."[3]

However, not all of his critics felt exactly the same way about Pfautsch's choral accomplishments. Pfautsch still remembers that every time his parents would visit Illinois Wesleyan for one of his choral concerts the response was always the same: "Well, that was very nice, Lloyd, but isn't it about time you quit university work and sought ordination for full-time work in the church? When are you going to return to church work?"

Pfautsch was also a promoter of collegiality among the voice faculty at IWU. He recalls that when Harry Robert Wilson visited his campus and had lunch with Pfautsch and the chair of the voice department, he was shocked to learn that the voice faculty held regular lunch meetings to discuss the needs of the department. "Wait a minute, did you say your voice department actually has meetings?" the famous conductor/arranger asked. "I don't believe it! I've never heard of the voice faculty at any university having meetings! They are always known as the war department of the Music division." Such was not true at IWU, however. Later Pfautsch was to attempt to achieve the same collegiality among the voice faculty at SMU, but with a bit less success.

While Pfautsch was establishing his reputation as a superb choral director, he also was launching his career as a published composer. As with conducting, he had been composing in a casual manner since high school, "back when I really didn't know what I was doing." By this time, however, he did know what he was doing. In 1948 he told a reporter for the IWU campus newspaper that "his hobbies included sports such as football, basketball, and especially baseball" and that "in his few spare minutes he enjoyed golfing and composing."[4] Composing soon became more of a regular activity and less of a hobby. Even his first Christmas concert at IWU included a piece he wrote for the occasion in the Aeolian mode, "Sing in Excelsis Gloria!" In 1951 Don Malin, an important choral music editor for C. C. Birchard, came to the Bloomington campus. He met Pfautsch in his studio and asked to look at some of his compositions. He was shown several and asked if he could take a few with him back to the publishing house. The result was that shortly thereafter Pfautsch received contracts for several anthems. He was paid the 10 percent fee expected by established composers, rather than a flat fee (often only $25 to $35) normally offered to unpublished writers. The first result was the publication of "Sing in Excelsis Gloria!" in 1951. *Five Narrative Carols*, which he had written for a newly formed women's chorus at IWU, and "Puer Nobis," the carol he had written as a class project for Harold Friedell, followed in 1953.

The *Five Narrative Carols* are typically Pfautschian with extensive use of *a cappella* singing, rhythms driven by text and a very simple but elegant accompaniment. They are scored for SSA choir and flute with an optional drum. The texture is varied in some by the addition of solo lines. No. 5 makes extensive use of unison chorus before dividing into SSA parts.

Pfautsch's first nine published works were all with C. C. Birchard. He felt grateful to Don Malin for giving him his start. He admitted having submitted compositions to other choral publishers (among them G. Schirmer, Carl Fischer, J. Fischer, and H. W. Gray) and receiving the usual polite letter saying, "we don't have room for this in our catalogue" or "we don't feel this would serve our catalogue." Later, when his published works were selling well, most of those other publishers approached him and offered to consider anything he might want to submit. But he wrote back that they had turned him down when he came to them and he preferred to stay with the two or three publishers who had helped him get established. If nothing else, it was a moral victory for the choral composer with the rapidly rising reputation. But eventually, grace and tact returned and he reconciled his self-righteous feelings and published at least one anthem with each of the aforementioned publishers.

The neophyte composer also received help and encouragement from Normand Lockwood, already an established composer, who was teaching at Trinity University in San Antonio, Texas. During a visit to the IWU campus, Lockwood looked at one of Pfautsch's carols and said, "You ought to have this published. I hate to say that to you, though, because Christmas carols are among the most difficult pieces to get published. If they don't like yours they will say that

Ex. 5 Five Narrative Carols, No. 1, 1953

they already have a heavy listing of carols in their catalog or that they already have a setting of that text. But if they do like it you will get an immediate reply with a contract and the music will be out shortly, certainly in time to hit the Christmas sales." Pfautsch found this to be quite true. He was, in fact, able to publish several carols through the years. He also wrote a number of carols for other seasons of the year: "A Time Carol" (1958), "A Carol for Thanksgiving" (1981), "A Carol for Advent" (1988), "A Carol for Palm Sunday" (1988), "A Carol for Ascension" (1988), "A Carol of Commitment" (1990), "A Carol for Pentecost" (1990), "A Carol for Easter" (1991), "A Carol for Epiphany" (1991), and a second "Carol for Thanksgiving" (1991). With the exception of the Epiphany carol those for other seasons have not sold especially well. The general public, including many musicians, think carols only belong to the Christmas season, despite historical evidence to the contrary.

Normand Lockwood, already a successful composer, did more for Pfautsch than just dispense advice. He also wrote a letter of introduction to Marjorie Farmer, his editor at Shawnee Press, urging her to carefully look over any manuscripts that Pfautsch might send her way because he was sure she would be interested in them.[5] Farmer took Lockwood's advice and published several works by Pfautsch in the last half of the 1950s.

The third major publisher of Pfautsch's music was Lawson-Gould in New York City. So much of his music was published there that many people thought he had an exclusive contract with Lawson-Gould. In truth he published with thirty different firms and just over one-third of his works are Lawson-Gould publications. Lawson-Gould was founded as a partnership between Robert Lawson Shaw and Walter Gould. Gould was Shaw's personal manager from the founding of the Robert Shaw Chorale until the maestro's death. Originally the company was to be called Lawson-Kent, Ltd. Kent was Shaw's grandmother's name. But Gould made a deal with Gus Schirmer to act as sales representative for the firm and it was Schirmer who suggested that Gould include his own last name in it. "People like to talk with someone whose name is in the title," Schirmer reasoned.[6] So Gould agreed to use his name, since he would be handling the business end of things. Also, Gould was the brother of famed composer/conductor Morton Gould, which helped lend some name-recognition to the fledgling company.

Gould and Shaw established the company as a way of promoting good choral music. Gould wanted to start with the top names in professional choral circles. At that time (1954) the three top American choral conductors were Robert Shaw, Roger Wagner, and Leonard DePaur. Of these Gould did not know Wagner, but Shaw did. So a dinner was arranged when Wagner stopped in New York on his way to England for a conducting engagement. Gould recalled dinner at a small Chinese restaurant on Sixth Avenue and 57th Street. Gould described the proposed publishing venture and Wagner agreed to be a part of it. He met separately with DePaur, who lived in New York and was therefore more accessible. DePaur first asked: "are you going to tell me what to write?" "No," came the reply, "we will publish what you would like us to publish, but if it's too difficult it will not sell." Gould found that, unfortunately, DePaur wrote very high voice parts, especially for tenors, and so not many choirs could perform his arrangements, even though they were exciting and well written. After achieving success with choral arrangements from the "big three" of choral music, Gould naturally added Alice Parker, who collaborated with Robert Shaw on most of the arrangements bearing his name and Sally Terri, who did likewise with Roger Wagner. The next tier to be added to the catalogue included Lloyd Pfautsch, Robert DeCormier, and Ralph Hunter.

One might assume that Robert Shaw was the initial connection between Gould and Pfautsch, but it was actually Clayton Krehbiel, who had sung with Shaw from the start and was a good friend of all three men. Krehbiel told Gould he should look into the music of Pfautsch. Krehbiel and Pfautsch were at a Music Educators National Conference in St. Louis when he made a point of introducing Pfautsch to Gould. Gould said to Lloyd, "Well, send me some music!" It probably did not hurt that Pfautsch also had a prior connection to Shaw. Whatever the case, by the second year of operation Gould's firm obtained manuscripts from Pfautsch and started publishing them. The first one out, *Songs Mein Grossmama Sang* (1956) is still one of Pfautsch's top sellers of all time. It is both clever and appealing, especially to choral musicians. Pfautsch conceived the idea of combining the fractured German of writer Dave Mora with musical parodies of the Brahms *Liebeslieder Waltzer*. He remembers getting the idea just before the IWU Collegiate Choir went on tour. He dashed off two of them and could hardly wait to get back home to complete the other two. Pfautsch felt that most of his best work came that way—very quickly and more or less all at once. The work is dedicated to "Bob and Eleven Co-waltzers," a reference to the select group of twelve singers Shaw used to record the Brahms work when Lloyd was still in New York. Each movement is a parody of a particular Brahms movement: No. 1, "Fraulein Bo-Peepen" closely parallels waltz No. 1, "Rede, Mächen, allzu lieber." No. 2, "Jack der Spratt," borrows from waltz No. 2, "Am Gesteine rauscht die Flut." No. 3, "Jack und Jill," draws on waltz No. 14 and no. 4, "Johann Horner," parodies waltz No. 18.

Grossmama was far from the only secular work Pfautsch published. In fact, as a university musician he felt it was important to give time to both secular and sacred music. About 20 percent of his published works have secular texts. One of the typically clever early efforts was written soon after he arrived at Illinois Wesleyan. It was the 100th anniversary of the university and he and another faculty member wrote music for an historical drama about the school. For

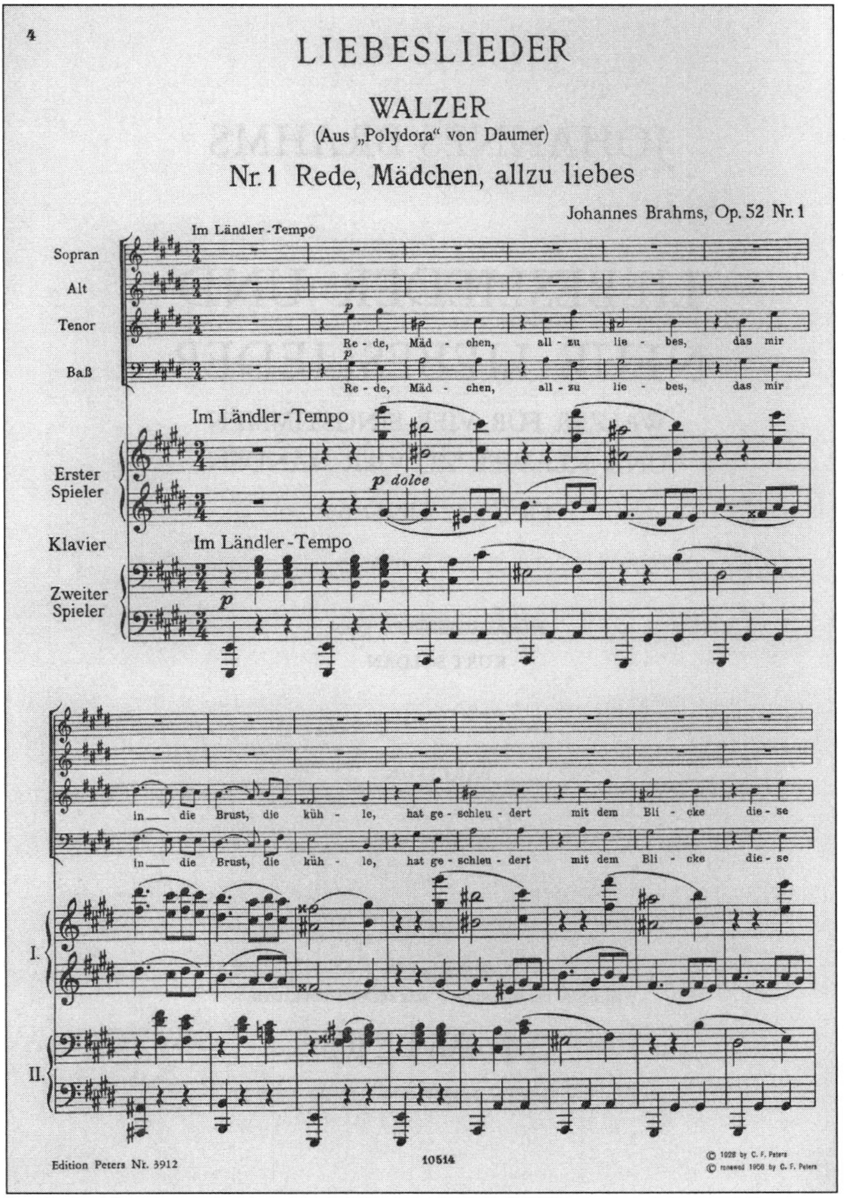

Ex. 6a Brahms *Liebeslieder Waltzer, No. 1*

Ex. 6b Songs Mein Grossmama Sang, 1956

a picnic scene in the late 1880s he wrote the medley "Jimmie Nags Jeannie," combining "Jimmy Crack Corn" (Abraham Lincoln's favorite) with "Camptown Races" ("nags") and Stephen Foster's "I Dream of Jeannie with the Light Brown Hair." Although the piece was published in 1955, as an occasional piece it did not sell all that well. It has experienced some performances since but deserves more, as it is both clever and well-crafted.

Walter Gould considers his 1976 work "Laughing Song" to be a fine example of Pfautsch's successful secular compositions. He called it "a very, very good selling piece." Gould continued, "Lloyd did very well from the standpoint of sales and performances. In fact, he still does."[7]

Gould and Pfautsch shared a mutual admiration, a somewhat rare relationship between creator and publisher, which lasted for over forty-five years. "I started publishing Lloyd's music in my second year of the business," Gould reminisced, "and I continued to do so until the very end, when I sold the company." Pfautsch commented on his publisher to this writer: "You will never meet a nicer man in your whole life than Walter Gould." As for their working relationship Gould recalled: "Lloyd was always a very prolific writer and it was a pleasure to work with him. He was really so knowing about so many areas and I can not say enough about him. And, I might add, of his wife Edie, a wonderful person!" Pfautsch said of Gould, "I owe him so much, really—the opportunities that he provided for me and his willingness to take a chance on some of the pieces, too. Some of them failed, some were risky, like *Day for Dancing*. Gould had never published anything like that before." Gould summed up his feelings about Pfautsch with: "I have to say what I said at the beginning, Lloyd is a very unusual human being; he's warm, he's concerned and he's just a talented man that deserves everything [good] that might come his way to be there. And, hopefully, to always be there."

It has been the experience of many choral conductors, including this writer, that men's glee clubs have more natural audience appeal than do women's glee clubs. It is ironic, though, that there is generally much better literature for women's groups. Part of this is because the voice ranges do not have to be so compressed when writing in the soprano/alto range and so it is easier to achieve a pleasing musical result in the treble clef. For similar reasons it is easier to adapt SATB music to SSAA. In spite of acknowledging the audience preference for male sounds, Pfautsch was always a champion of music for women's voices. Of the first ten pieces he published, four are for SATB, four are for women's voices, and only two are for men's voices. Soon after he arrived at Illinois Wesleyan he started a women's chorus and began writing music for them. One example is his second publication, *Five Narrative Carols* for SSA, flute, and drum (ex. 5 above).

Pfautsch wrote one of his most successful sellers for children's choirs. Not many of his works were written for choirs other than his own (except for commissions, of course), but his SA arrangement of Psalm 23 set as a spiritual was published in 1957 and has been popular ever since. He thought the chance for children to sing this well-known Psalm with a different translation and versification was important. Children's choir directors since then have agreed with him. The piece is both beautiful and practical. Although he wrote a descant for the final verse ("I will fear no evil"), it is optional. The spiritual melody is folk-like and easy to learn. It employs a narrow range of pitches, one that is ideal for young voices (from E above middle C up to the C# above that). The simple beauty of this work is a testament to its composer's skill and talent.

Pfautsch wrote other music for junior choir as well, including the 1964 Chorister's Guild publication "A Child's Prayer," the 1964 col-

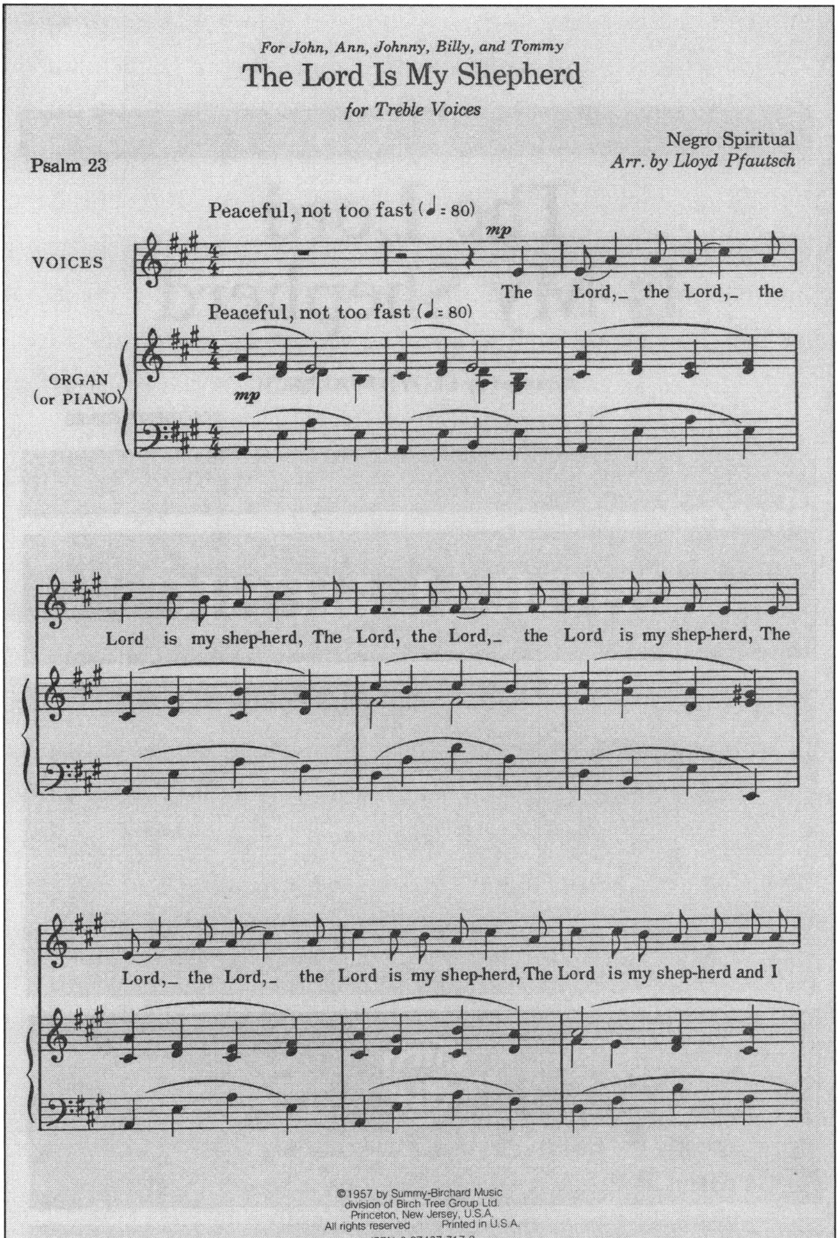

Ex. 7 The Lord is my Shepherd, 1957

lection from Abingdon Press, *Six Anthems for Junior Choir*, and the 1972 anthem, "A Carol for Children," using a text by Ogden Nash.

A lifelong champion of new choral music, Pfautsch was directly involved in the commissioning of new works in two important ways. In 1952 he convinced the Illinois Wesleyan University administration to fund the Collegiate Choir Commission Series. The first work commissioned was Earl George's *Songs of Innocence*. The plan was that the choir would premiere the new work on campus and then sing it on tour in the spring of that year. In the hopes of attracting wider audiences, sacred and secular texts were chosen in alternate years. Some of the composers were unknown, but promising. Others, such as Anthony Donato, Burrill Phillips, Ulysses Kay, Leo Sowerby, Normand Lockwood, Jean Berger, and John Joubert, were already established names in the field. Although Pfautsch could never find a publisher willing to agree to take on the commissioned works as a series, at least half of them were published on their own. In fact, Pfautsch pointed out, the Earl George work is not only one of his most popular pieces, it was also one of Summy-Birchard's best-sellers.

When Pfautsch took the George pieces on tour that year he got a very favorable review of his Chicago performance at Kimball Hall:

> Illinois Wesleyan University brought its choir to Kimball Hall on March 28 [1952] for its annual concert under the direction of Lloyd Pfautsch. The conductor and his group achieved excellent results in matters of balance, ensemble and phrasing. The program was selected with impeccable taste and imagination. Of particular interest were five short poems from Blake's *Songs of Innocence* set with guileless charm by Earl George, on commission from the choir.[8]

The second way in which Pfautsch was involved in commissioned choral music is that he himself was asked to write many works on commission. His first one was "Spring," written in 1956 for the Sigma Alpha Iota Chapter at IWU. It was published by M. Witmark. In all, Pfautsch produced ninety-two commissioned works. What is even more remarkable is that eighty of them (87 percent) were published! By their very nature commissioned works, like bridesmaid's dresses, tend to be occasional in nature and so it is usually quite difficult to find uses for them (or get them published) after their initial performance. But Pfautsch had the knack of writing music appropriate to the occasion that was also suitable for wider uses and therefore appealed to publishers and their customers.[9]

These two types of involvement with new choral music converged when Pfautsch was asked to write the twenty-fifth commissioned work for the IWU Collegiate Choir Series in 1978. In a speech on the IWU campus when his new work was presented, Pfautsch talked about his purposes in establishing the series:

> First of all, there was the desire to encourage young, unknown American composers to write for choral ensembles. . . . Secondly, there was the desire to enlarge the repertoire available for choral ensembles to perform. Third was to provide new settings for old and familiar texts as well as settings of texts that had not been previously set for choirs. A fourth purpose involved an emphasis on varieties of style, the exploitation of new and developing contemporary or avant-garde compositional techniques. A fifth purpose was the hope that this new repertoire would be of service to both school and church choral ensembles and thus on alternate years sacred and secular texts were to alternate.[10]

In a salute to the first commissioned piece by Earl George, Pfautsch wrote *Songs of Experience*. Not only were they meant as a foil to George's *Songs of Innocence*, but he also parodied George's

The Lamb in his "Be Careful What You Say." The three movements in Pfautsch's work were appropriate in other ways as well. His first movement used a text by Charles Wesley, emphasizing the university's Methodist roots. The second movement had the George reference, but also employed a text by Carl Sandberg, arguably Illinois's greatest poet. And the final movement used a text by Adlai Stevenson, who was raised in Bloomington and whose family ran the *Pantagon-Dispatch* in that city. The text was taken from his acceptance speech at the Democratic National Convention in Chicago when he was first nominated as their candidate for president of the United States. The speech was in the form of a litany and was so well-received that it ran on page one of *The New York Times* the following day. Both Pfautsch's and George's works were performed at the Founders Convocation of 1978 and both composers were present. Pfautsch was asked to give the keynote address, discussing "The Establishment of the Collegiate Choir Commission Series." He was then awarded the honorary Doctor of Humane Letters by his former institution of employment. It served as a warm and reaffirming reminder of his many happy years on the IWU campus.

In October of 1977 Pfautsch sent an advanced copy of his S*ongs of Experience* to George. In return George wrote a letter of appreciation on October 26, 1977: "I can't tell you how pleased—and touched—and honored!—I was to get the copy of 'Songs of Experience.' It's only natural that I should be most fascinated by the setting of 'The Lamb' (what an idea – and how tastefully done) but I was equally taken by the two others as well; Adlai Stevenson happens to be one of my particular heroes, and you've found just the right tone for his words." After the anniversary celebration at IWU, Earl sent another letter to Pfautsch dated April 2, 1978. This one included his comments on the gala celebration: "to thank you for your nice words, and to tell you how great it was for us to see you and Edie again—and to be able to be present to see you receive at least something like your just reward (they haven't invented a degree that will do that!) I hope I made it clear how much I liked your SOE! and how touched I was by the relationship it has to my ancient effort."[11]

That commissioned series was an excellent source of contacts for Pfautsch as he continued to build his strong reputation in national music circles. Although he did not write a piece for the series, Aaron Copland was invited to campus as their featured composer one year. Pfautsch narrated *A Lincoln Portrait* with the orchestra and the choir sang his setting of Gertrude Stein's "Sing We for Love and Idleness," among other works. In both cases the famous composer let him know that he was not entirely pleased with the performances. He preferred that the narration be delivered matter-of-factly and not dramatically as Pfautsch had done. Copland told him directly that he liked the last page of the Stein setting to be done considerably faster than he had taken it. Finally, as they were sitting in the station waiting for the train to take Copland back to New York he mentioned that he could always tell when a composer was a pianist by the way he writes for the piano. Pfautsch held his tongue but was tempted to say, "and I can always tell when the composer is a singer or understands the human voice by the way he writes for it." Pfautsch had recently made special arrangements for one of his prize voice students to sing Copland's yet unpublished Emily Dickinson songs on her senior recital and found that the voice was often treated in a manner better suited to instrumental writing.

He also received advice and correspondence from other musical luminaries while at Illinois Wesleyan. Among them was Ralph Vaughan Williams, who sent a very polite "no" when asked to accept a commission for the Collegiate Choir Series.[12] Then, too, a recital at

IWU by Antwerp organist/composer Flor Peters resulted in a friendship between the two composers.[13] Mention already has been made of Normand Lockwood's kind assistance to Pfautsch after a visit to IWU when his commissioned work was premiered. Pfautsch's contact with University of Illinois composer Burrill Phillips when his work was performed at IWU led to a relationship in which Pfautsch eventually studied composition with Phillips during the year he taught at the University of Illinois.

Text was always the starting point for Lloyd Pfautsch's composition. He was quite intentional about that and called his writing *logogenic*: "I believe that all vocal music should be *logogenic*. The word is the most important thing. I don't believe in forcing the text to fit musical ideas or melodic ideas." Whether it was the profound thoughts of a Medieval or Renaissance writer (*Prayer of St. Francis*) or the fractured German of Dave Mora (*Songs Mein Grossmama Sang*) he first got inspiration from the words and then conceived music to enhance their innate rhythms and meanings. In addition to Mora one of his frequent secular sources was the children's poetry of Ebil Arlene ("A Time Carol," *et al.*) His primary sacred source, of course, was the Holy Bible. In general his seminary education influenced his ability to exegete a biblical passage, but he was particularly inspired by two of his professors at Union Seminary: The first was James Meilenburg, whose flowing white hair and passion for teaching the Old Testament writers gave his students the impression they were studying the Bible with Moses himself. The second, Samuel Terrien, was both a knowledgeable musician and one of the greatest living experts on the Book of Psalms. Most of the time Pfautsch considered this influence to have been subconscious; he absorbed the studies and they simply became a part of him. Examples of this influence easily can be found in his effective and appropriate settings of "The Temptation of Christ" (1961), "The Annunciation" (1972), and "Isaiah's Vision" (1976). His former mentor, Terrien, commented favorably on all of these Bible-based works, but was especially taken with "Isaiah's Vision." Pfautsch said, "I'll admit that Terrien's exegesis came into play a number of times. Exegesis does play a role in all of my settings of Biblical texts. I hope that when people listen to the text it takes on a little different meaning for them because of that." Clearly Pfautsch understood the prophetic nature of sacred music and hoped his settings enhanced that aspect of music in worship.

In 1956, Pfautsch was invited to seek a leave of absence from IWU and serve as visiting director of choral activities at the University of Illinois. It was a year he remembered with very mixed emotions. When he was hired as a visiting professor of music, Dean Duane Brannigan told him, "Frankly, I think it'll be just a matter of course. I can't say now that you will be appointed permanent Director of Choral Activities, but if everything goes right, you'll just stay on."[14] So Pfautsch moved his growing family to Champaign and applied his now perfected combination of hard work and choral expertise to developing several fine choirs who respected him and also assumed he was to be their permanent conductor.

His biggest challenge was to prepare his choirs for the Biennial Contemporary Music Symposium for which the conductor was to be Robert Shaw. Just before Shaw arrived, Dean Brannigan came out to Pfautsch's house to pay him a visit, but it was not a social call. The dean informed Pfautsch that he had decided to hire his friend and former classmate at Oberlin Conservatory, Harold Decker, as the permanent director of choral activities. Decker was then teaching at Wichita State University in Kansas. Pfautsch was more than taken aback, but he had the presence of mind to say, "Duane, what I suspected has been borne out to be true. You were just using me this year. You had Shaw coming for the symposium to conduct the orchestra and the choral ensembles and you wanted to be sure you had somebody who knew how to work for Robert." Pfautsch had nailed him and the dean admitted he was right, but it still hurt. He had one flash of moral victory a few days later when he happened to be in the hallway of the music building and observed an associate dean reading a clipping from a Wichita paper announcing that Decker was coming to the university. The administrator read the clipping, tore it down from the bulletin board, wadded it up, tossed it in the trash, and angrily walked on down the hallway. Frankly, many in the choral community known to this writer felt that the dean's decision was both unfair and unwise.

When Robert Shaw came to Illinois for the symposium, his reaction to Pfautsch's situation was "If I'd known that [*you were being used*] I wouldn't have come." But in his typically loyal manner Shaw bent over backwards to be kind to Pfautsch while he was there. He was very complimentary of each of the choral groups, both privately and publicly. In each rehearsal of the new works for choir and orchestra he was able to deal with the choir and make his corrections and suggestions in a relatively short time and then excuse the choir so he could concentrate on the orchestra. All of his interviews with the local media included favorable comments about the various choirs at the university: "The Men's Glee Club, in fact all the choral societies here, are wonderful groups. The School of Music has a marvelous group of instructors, especially Lloyd Pfautsch and Bernard Goodman."[15] When Shaw attended Pfautsch's conducting class, Lloyd introduced him by saying: "When I was in college there was a wise professor of mine from Germany who told us 'There will be times in your life when you will encounter people who are famous and whom you know to be great by reputation but you will only fully appreciate their greatness when you are actually in their presence.' At the time I wondered what he was saying. But I finally understood when my wife and I were in rehearsal with the NBC Chorus and Arturo Toscanini suddenly walked in. Then I *knew* what my professor meant. And the other times I have felt that way are each of the times I am in the presence of Robert Shaw and working with him." Shaw's self-effacing reaction was "You sure are full of bull sometimes!" But Pfautsch was happy to have had the opportunity to tell Shaw how he felt in front of the choir. He also had a chance to play a recording of his *Songs Mein Grossmama Sang* when the maestro was out at his house relaxing over a few beers after a long rehearsal with the university ensembles. Shaw was delighted with what he heard and appreciated the dedication "To Bob and Eleven Co-waltzers." Somehow after that week sales of the work, although already doing well, seemed to skyrocket. Shaw's support for Pfautsch never wavered either then or in the subsequent years until the elder maestro's death.

Upon his return home Shaw sent a hand-written note to Pfautsch:

> Dear Lloyd—
>
> Again—many thanks for the courtesies unlimited of the Festival Choir at Urbana.
>
> Was fine to see you again and hear your fine work, alive and recorded.
>
> Home in Scarsdale now and about to start a hectic recording schedule.
>
> John Thaddeus is a wonder! Enjoying him extravagantly.
>
> Best always,
>
> Bob[16]

In his conducting class at the University of Illinois, Pfautsch had the unusual pleasure of teaching two doctoral students who were orchestral conductors. It is one of the anomalies of the music world that most choral conductors understand the need to undertake the study of instrumental conducting before facing an instrumental ensemble but few orchestral conductors, even at the highest levels, see the need to study voice or choral conducting before working with vocal ensembles. The very few who are trained in both (for example Robert Shaw and Simon Rattle) do an obviously superior job when conducting choral symphonies, oratorios, operas, and cantatas. In most universities choral conducting graduate students are required to take at least one course in instrumental conducting but the reverse is seldom if ever true. Also part of the problem with developing first-rate choral conductors in this country is that the glamour and salary go to instrumental conductors. As Walter Gould observed, "we do not have too many really good choral conductors emerging. It does not pay well. There are so many areas where people can make so much more money, that you just have to say 'This is what I love, and it's what I want to stay with.'"

But for Pfautsch and his two instrumental conducting students the classroom situation proved to be mutually beneficial. After attending class and watching his choral rehearsals for a few weeks the two men approached Prof. Pfautsch and said: "We've been watching you in rehearsal with the choirs and we notice that you use certain gestures that seem to indicate something to the chorus to help them. We don't know what, but we notice that the diction gets better when you do it!" So Pfautsch thought about this and as he conducted rehearsals that week he enlisted what he called "my *doppelgänger*" to observe himself. He discovered that without intentionally doing so, he had developed an empathy with the singers such that variations of his beat pattern technique enabled him to indicate what consonant he wanted and where he wanted it placed; how to sing that conso-

Choir rehearsal at Illinois Wesleyan.

nant at the beginning, middle or ending of a phrase. So Pfautsch began to be more intentional about this conducting technique and learned, through work with his students, how to teach it to them.[17]

Once again the ideal educational situation arose: teacher and students learning from one another.

That year Pfautsch was also a student of composition. He asked Burrill Phillips from the School of Music's composition department to take him on as a student for the year. In their first session Phillips said to him, "Why don't you write something for the piano?" Lloyd replied, "I'd feel very uncomfortable, I'm not a pianist." But the teacher persisted: "Well I think you ought to try. Just put your hands down on the piano like this (Phillips randomly struck B, F sharp, G sharp, A sharp, and C natural) and see what you can do with that." The result was *Dancetudes*, three short dances for piano solo. Although Phillips was encouraging, Pfautsch never did try to get them published and he continued to feel reticent about his writing for keyboard, especially for the accompaniments to his choral pieces. As renowned composer and former student, Jane Marshall, points out, "None of us who are keyboard players find anything wrong with them, but Lloyd does."[18]

Pfautsch spent the rest of the year writing choral music for Phillips. Included in that effort is another unpublished work, "Thy Temple Stands to Serve," which he wrote for the dedication of St. Peter's Evangelical and Reformed Church in Champaign (1957), the church he and his family attended while living there. But Pfautsch also decided to write an anthem based on a prayer by his mentor at Union Theological Seminary, Reinhold Niebuhr. Even though Niebuhr's fame was worldwide, he told Lloyd that he was the first one ever to ask to set any of his words to music! Niebuhr graciously granted permission to use the text and replied enthusiastically when Pfautsch sent him a copy of the manuscript: "I am very grateful to you for doing this."[19] The work was published by Lawson-Gould in 1958 as "Invocation." Pfautsch later wished he could change the title

Publicity photo during the Illinois Wesleyan years.

to "Serenity," by which the prayer is generally known. It was reissued as "The Serenity Prayer" by Abingdon Press in 2003. As his composition teacher, Lloyd found Phillips to be very helpful and to be sensitive about text in the same way he was. Pfautsch summed up the pupil-teacher relationship with: "we got along very well." Even a year after his study with Phillips (in a letter dated Dec. 2, 1959) Phillips praised two new manuscripts from Pfautsch as follows:

> I am particularly pleased with the CHRIST FOUNDATION, HEAD AND CORNERSTONE setting. I think

> that in both you have used the brass with distinction and taste. The quality of the music comes through as being your own style—I can so easily see the kind of rhythmic treatment that is a distinguishing mark of your writing, and a very refreshing one at that. You should have a real success with these, as I think they are both practicable and very interesting. Are they to be published?

After a demanding, often-fulfilling but unpredictable year as visiting director of choral activities at the University of Illinois, Pfautsch and his family moved back to Bloomington and Illinois Wesleyan University. While he had learned a lot, both about conducting and about composition, and had developed some excellent choral organizations, he had also had to face a major disappointment. He returned to IWU for what was to be his final year among those friends, colleagues, and admirers. He had thoroughly enjoyed the years in Bloomington, but now, after a decade, it was time to move to Texas and reach the fulfillment of all of his years of preparation, learning, and achievement. He again felt a call and responded favorably when he was asked to inaugurate a new graduate program in Sacred Music at Southern Methodist University. The unique degree was to be jointly sponsored by the School of Music and the School of Theology and Pfautsch eagerly accepted this challenge to his creativity, moving his family for the third time in three years, this time to Dallas, Texas. Thankfully, It was the family's final move until the children grew up and moved out of their parents' house at 3710 Euclid Avenue in the town of Highland Park, within walking distance of the SMU campus.

Chapter 4

The Dance of Fulfillment

(Texas)

LLOYD PFAUTSCH CAME TO TEXAS for a job incorporating both theology and music, finally resolving the tensions he had faced since high school days in trying to choose one field over the other. Attempting to fulfill his parents' dream of a son ordained by the church and still satisfy his own creative urges as a musician had been a constant anxiety for at least twenty years. The Master of Sacred Music program required knowledge and skill in both theology and music and the new director was expected to qualify for tenure on both faculties. At the time Pfautsch moved to Dallas, the Music Department at SMU was about the same size as that at Illinois Wesleyan, so, in one sense, it was a lateral move. But he was drawn to SMU primarily for the challenge of designing and implementing their new sacred music program. He also realized it was time to move on from the Illinois school where he had accomplished most of the goals he had set for himself. Further, it was no small consideration that he would at last hold a faculty position in a seminary and could, therefore, qualify for ordination according to the rules of the United Church of Christ, the successor to the Evangelical and Reformed Church of his youth. He was ordained in his home church in Washington, Missouri, at the end of his first year in Texas (1959).

The Pfautsch family settled into a lovely home at 3710 Euclid Avenue in Highland Park. Highland Park and University Park, collectively known as the Park Cities, are incorporated cities surrounded on all sides by the City of Dallas. Southern Methodist University is mainly in the Park Cities as well. At the time, Pfautsch felt really stretched to meet the mortgage payments for that house, because his salary at SMU was not very much more than he had been making at IWU. When he retired, however, he reaped the benefits of this choice, as he sold the property for many times what he paid for it. He told this writer in 1988 that his taxes that year on the Euclid house were more than his mortgage payments had been when he moved there. In fact, after retirement he was able to buy another very nice house still in the Park Cities for cash and also deposit a significant profit from the sale of the Euclid home to his retirement account. While his house was within walking distance of the university, it also put the Pfautsch children into the unique Highland Park school system. It was not until they were adults that they told their parents how unhappy they had been in the totally segregated school system. They found it difficult being among the very few children who did not come from the economic upper class and did not have every latest fashion and every hot new toy or car or other material pleasure. They also did not share values with many of their classmates. They did not view an all-Caucasian environment as desirable, for example. Somehow the Pfautsches managed to raise their children with broader interests and a more enlightened social understanding than

Photos shot during a performance by the Illinois Wesleyan Choir.

were generally associated with a Park Cities education in that era. At that time, it was more feasible for SMU faculty to live in the Park Cities than it is today, so there were some other students in the same financial and philosophical boat as the Pfautsch children. No doubt this helped to some extent. Two other students of the time known to this writer have expressed similar views. Today, incidentally, most faculty at the university live in other areas of the Dallas/Fort Worth metroplex, some as far as twenty-five miles away!

The development of a Master of Sacred Music program at Southern Methodist University was the result of a distinguished and forward-thinking convocation of experts in education and church music from around the United States. In November of 1955, some three years before Pfautsch was called to teach at SMU, Deans Cuninggim (Theology) and Borchers (Music) called a panel from throughout the nation to spend two days at SMU discussing the creation of the proposed degree program. In addition to the two SMU deans, other administrators included were: Earl E. Harper (dean, School of Music, University of Iowa), David Hugh Jones (Music Department chair, Princeton University), Henry Meyer (dean, School of Music, Southwestern University, TX), Hugh Porter (director of the School of Sacred Music at Union Theological Seminary, NYC), and John Finley Williamson (founder and president, Westminster Choir College). Prominent church musicians invited were Nita Akin (organist, First Methodist, Wichita Falls, Texas, and adjunct professor of organ at Mid-America University), Temple Barcafer (music minister, Tyler Street Methodist, Dallas), Norman Blake (St. Mark's School, Dallas), Robert Clark (First Methodist, Fort Worth), Meredith Cravens (director of education and music, First UMC, Little Rock), Glen Johnson (music minister, Lovers Lane Methodist, Dallas), Cecil Lapo (music minister, St. Luke's, Tulsa, Oklahoma), Austin Lovelace (minister of music, First Methodist, Evanston, Illinois, and president, Fellowship of Methodist Musicians), David McCormick (organist, Highland Park Methodist, Dallas), and Federal Lee Whittlesey (music minister, Highland Park Methodist, Dallas). University faculty represented were George Baker (theology), Dora Poteet Barclay (music and university organist), Dorothy Ellsworth (wife of Gene and children's music specialist), Eugene Ellsworth (music), Fred Gealy (theology), and Joseph Quillian (theology; subsequent dean of theology). Panel membership was completed with Jake Akin (philanthropist; husband of Nita), Ruth Krehbiel Jacobs (founder, Choristers Guild), and Walter Towner (Methodist Board of Education, Nashville). In the annals of American sacred music this was undoubtedly a unique gathering. Although there were important differences of opinion from such a varied and experienced group of musicians and educators, they still unanimously concluded that starting such a program as the Master of Sacred Music degree was a very worthwhile endeavor and should be pursued.

The work of creating the degree then moved to SMU itself, and to Pfautsch once he joined the faculty. Chairing the committee to develop a curriculum for the new graduate program in sacred music proved to be both challenging and fulfilling for Professor Pfautsch. The committee included one dean and two faculty from each of the schools (music and theology) plus Pfautsch. This seven-man group met every Friday throughout the academic year 1958–59. The influence of Union Theological Seminary was pervasive in these sessions. Like Pfautsch, many of the Perkins faculty had been Union graduates. Then, too, Pfautsch's MSM thesis, "A Curriculum of Church Music for a Theological Seminary . . . ," no doubt came into play.[1] Finally, the nationally recognized Master of Sacred Music program at Union was, to a large extent, the model for this new program. Both programs consisted of sixty semester hours to be completed in two years with course work taken from the curriculums of both disciplines. However, the situation at SMU was a bit different from that at Union. First of all, this was a university setting and not a self-contained seminary. Two separate schools of the university were involved on a more or less equal basis in creating and approving this degree. While both the theology school and the music school faculties wanted the program to proceed, neither understood much at all about how the other operated. For example, students were matriculating with adequate preparation to start graduate work in music but with little, if any, preparation in biblical and theological studies. In the beginning, the theology representatives wanted the course work to be evenly divided between the two schools. Eventually they came to understand that it was unrealistic to expect these students to complete thirty credit hours in theology as well as their music studies. In the end they compromised on thirty-eight to forty semester hours of music courses and twenty-two semester hours of theology studies. It was stipulated that the theology courses would be those from the regular course schedule and that students from all of the theology degree programs would take these classes together. This latter stipulation was inspired by the largely successful way in which Union had integrated music and theology students by putting them together in several academic courses. At Union many of them also lived in the same dormitories, sometimes as roommates, forming lifelong friendships. This also happened in Dallas during the nascent years of the degree program, but to a lesser extent.

The committee deciding the new curriculum included the two deans (Merrimon Cuninggim from theology and Orville Borchers from music) and Pfautsch, as well as two particularly supportive colleagues: Gene Ellsworth from the Music Theory faculty and Fred Gealy from the New Testament faculty. Ellsworth, like Pfautsch, held a Master of Sacred Music degree from Union Theological Seminary and so understood how that program worked. Gealy had amazingly diverse knowledge and skills. He had been a missionary to Japan as well as a professor and thus taught a course in world religions when he first came to SMU. In addition to that and teaching on the Bible faculty he also directed the Seminary Singers and was the organist-choirmaster at University Park United Methodist Church. The rumor at Perkins Seminary was that Gealy had actually taught every course ever offered by the seminary![2] Certainly he came close. Pfautsch considered him to be "a true Renaissance man." The other two equally compatible and supportive committee members were Herdon Wagers from theology and Farrold Stephens from music.

SMU had both the advantage and the challenge of creating a program between two existing schools of the same university. However, the response from the faculties of both schools was largely enthusiastic. This was answered by a positive response from the central administration and so the program was successfully launched. Pfautsch was, in fact, surprised at how easily and quickly the final version was approved by both faculties.

Because the new MSM students would primarily take courses that already existed in the two schools, it was assumed that the only cost involved would be that of Pfautsch's salary. His stipend was furnished in some combination by the two schools plus the Office of the Chaplain. The chaplain was involved because at the end of Pfautsch's first year at SMU it was decided to begin regular Sunday services in Perkins Chapel and Pfautsch was asked to organize and direct the Chapel Choir.

But of course each new degree program does need its own funding and the MSM program was no exception. Fortunately, Jake and Nita Akin of Wichita Falls were very much in favor of the program, having participated in the 1955 convocation at SMU that launched the development of the degree. For the first few years of the MSM's existence they gave $2000 annually to help it develop. At a time when tuition for the MSM degree was $300 per semester, this was a very handsome gift, indeed. Mr. Akin was a successful Texas oilman and his wife, Nita, was the long-time organist at First Methodist Church in Wichita Falls as well as a member of the music faculty at Mid-America University. Some of this money was used for scholarships and the rest went to operating expenses. Eventually the two schools at SMU realized that they must budget for this program and so they did.

Pfautsch's move to SMU affected his composition choices to some extent. For example he composed his first hymn-anthem shortly after moving to Dallas and assuming direction of the Perkins Chapel Choir. He set "Sing Praise to God" to the tune *Mit freuden zart* in 1959. He wrote it because he had introduced the tune to Claude Evans, then university chaplain, by choosing it as one of the hymns for a Sunday chapel service. He was completely dumbfounded when Evans, who liked it very much, said he had never heard it before. So Pfautsch wanted his chapel choir to sing his arrangement of the German chorale for a Sunday chapel service. It is dedicated to Claude Evans and his wife, Maxilla.

As he continued his work at Southern Methodist University, Pfautsch wrote many more hymn-tune arrangements including: "Come, Thou Fount of Every Blessing" (Warrenton, 1962); "I'll Praise My Maker" (Old 113th, 1982); "Praise to the Lord" (*Lobe den Herren*, 1990); "A Thousand Tongues to Sing" (Azmon and Richmond, 1990); and "Lord Jesus, Think on Me" (Southwell, 1996)[3] All but the last one were performed by the Chapel Choir and some by other choirs he directed.

Another example of the influence of his employment upon his composition choices might be seen in Pfautsch's use of chant or chant-like melodies for some pieces. "Come Holy Spirit" is a parody of the plainsong "*Veni, Sancte Spiritus.*" "Seek to Serve," on the other hand, employs a chant-like melody that was original with Pfautsch, albeit loosely based on the "*Kyrie*" from *Mass IX "Cum Jubilo."* The latter may well be the most widely useful anthem he wrote (see page 95). It is very beautiful, mostly employs unison writing, and sets a text that is appropriate many times throughout the church year. This writer has introduced this beautiful work to many choirs, both here and abroad, and it is universally admired by choristers and con-

Ex. 8 Sing Praise to God, 1959

gregations. Famed choral director Paul Salomunovich remarked to Pfautsch: "Hey, Lloyd, I'm sure glad you sent me that *Seek to Serve.* I use it at every workshop. It is a great piece for Catholic church musicians to use."[4] As almost any composer, writer, painter, sculptor, or choreographer will agree the most difficult art to create is art that is simple. It is less challenging to make a complex work of art. This little anthem wonderfully displays Pfautsch's great strength as a composer in that it is both simply beautiful and beautifully simple.

It is also significant that Pfautsch wrote all of his works for organ and organ with other instruments during his employment at SMU. As mentioned before, Pfautsch always regretted not having taken good advantage of the piano lessons his parents tried to provide for him in his youth. He felt throughout his career that he was not good at writing for the keyboard and so generally shied away from doing so. Further he always belittled the keyboard accompaniments he wrote for his anthems. That is one reason that many of his anthems use percussion or wind instruments instead of or in addition to keyboard as an accompaniment. Most choral musicians do not agree with Pfautsch's self-assessment, however.

Nevertheless, Pfautsch did write six works for organ. Of these only his *Three Organ Preludes on Hymn Tunes* (1965) is for organ solo. Pfautsch wrote quite varied settings of three rather obscure early American hymn tunes. Prelude I, "Garden Hymn" is a peaceful, pastoral counterpoint dedicated to Russell Miles and Paul Pettinga, organ instructors at the University of Illinois when Pfautsch taught there. The second movement, "The Converted Thief," employs the tune in the tenor voice with triadic writing for the right hand and a slow-moving pedal part that at times provides a counterpoint with the tenor. It is dedicated to Nita Akin, the first benefactrice of the MSM Program. Prelude III, "Warrenton" is a technically demanding

Ex. 9 Seek to Serve, 1983

work written for his former student and by then colleague, Robert Anderson. Anderson, who possessed a masterful keyboard technique, told Pfautsch he worked and worked on the piece for weeks, but was so upset with his first performance (at a Perkins Chapel Sunday morning service) that he stormed out of the chapel vowing, "I'm going to learn to play that piece right if it's the last thing I do!" He worked on it for three more weeks and played it again. This time he got through it without a hitch and afterwards slammed down the console lid and audibly sighed: "There, I made it through once accurately and I am never going to play this in public again!" Anderson's approach to music was nothing, if not dramatic!

Of the works for organ and instruments, two are among the very few extant works by Pfautsch that are unpublished. Both are settings of the Martin Luther hymn, *Ein' feste Burg*. The other three compositions for organ and instruments, all very successful pieces, are published and still receive performances. Of these "I'll Praise My Maker," a 1967 adaptation of his 1960 anthem, is the most popular. It uses organ, three trumpets, and two trombones. Perhaps the most interesting is his *Affirmation* (1975) for organ, percussion, and narrator. He was commissioned by organist Wilma Jenson and K. Dean Walker, percussionist, to write this piece. The duo performed many organ and percussion recitals and first used this work at a regional convention of the American Guild of Organists. The narrator's part is a poem by Emily Brontë. The composer had long been interested in that poem, but never felt a choral or vocal musical response to its rhythm and structure. Using it for the narration provided the perfect solution to his dilemma about how to set it.

Pfautsch also wrote occasional pieces for SMU, as one might expect. He harmonized the modest tune "Varsity" so his choirs could make the university song sound as well as possible at official academic and sports occasions. He also wrote a fascinating setting of Psalm 47 for the 1967 dedication of the Hastings Harrison Building (which was to house the Music Department). Hand-clapping in this work and other such body sounds were used several times by Pfautsch (e.g., Ex. 12a, b below). He found that with clapping there were two performance possibilities. Either the entire choir could memorize the music and thus have their hands free, or half the choir could hold scores so they and a partner could read them and only the half without scores would do the clapping. Pfautsch usually preferred the latter approach because he felt he still got plenty of sound this way but the reduced number clapping was easier to bring into a tight ensemble. This work, however, was one of the few where he preferred that everyone memorize the score and that all of the choir clap together, possibly because of the imperative in the first line of text ("Clap your hands!").

Faculty today would pale at the workload Pfautsch maintained in his early years at SMU, all of it in addition to the time spent composing! At a time when the senior faculty in theology taught six credit hours per semester and those in the other schools handled nine, Pfautsch taught nine hours each semester in the School of Theology, twelve hours in the School of Music and rehearsed and conducted the University Chapel Choir. During the week he led the Seminary Singers (a group of seventy men), the University Choir, the Choral Union, the Women's Chorus and, on Sunday, the Chapel Choir. The Seminary Singers and the University Choir each toured annually. In addition, he taught courses each semester in both schools, such as advanced conducting, advanced choral arranging, hymnology, and the history of music and worship. He found the last mentioned course a particular challenge since he had never taught anything like it before and had to do a lot of preparation in music history just to stay ahead

Ex. 10 Sing Praises

of the class! But Pfautsch was something of a workaholic and far from complaining about the workload demanded of him he valued the variety involved. When it was pointed out that his choirs took enormous amounts of time because each had different needs and different repertoire, he replied, "Yes, it was a valuable experience!"[5]

As if all of the above activities were not enough, Pfautsch also prepared the Dallas Opera Chorus for its 1960 season! This turned out to be a fortuitous endeavor because in December of that year it led to the formation of the Dallas Civic Chorus. Lloyd mentioned to the opera singers that it was a shame that a town the size of Dallas had no community chorus to represent the city. His chorus agreed and together about thirty of them formed the Dallas Civic Chorus. They started with what Pfautsch considered minor league programs (a lot of popular music, with a substantial work or two wedged in between). The spring concert for 1962, for example, started with the Hindemith *Four Chansons* followed by Dello Joio's "A Jubilant Song," but also included several spirituals, a Pfautsch piece or two, and selections from Rodgers and Hammerstein's *Carousel.* While most of the singers, including Edie Pfautsch, were trained musicians it was strictly an amateur ensemble in the sense that no one was paid to sing with the group, nor was the conductor paid. On the contrary, singers were assessed a modest dues each year to cover incidental expenses. Chorus members themselves sold most of the tickets for their concerts to earn enough money to pay the instrumental musicians from the Dallas Symphony as accompanists. This practice developed into a positive relationship with the DSO and the Dallas Civic Chorus was asked to sing with the DSO several times in those early years. Further, several symphony players told Pfautsch that they liked to play for his concerts, partly because he chose literature they would otherwise never get to play. He found that if rehearsal time was short he could not run overtime, due to union rules and a lack of funds. However, more than once he heard various instrumental sections "wood shedding" together after rehearsal until they got a difficult passage under control. The result was always a fine performance the next night. It was this bond of musical respect between players, conductor, and music that helped the performers achieve excellence on a shoestring budget. Pfautsch became so well-known among the symphony players that they later told him the standing joke on their previous summer's orchestra tour was to use his name as an expletive. If someone dropped a mouthpiece while cleaning it, for example, they would exclaim: "Oh, Pfautsch!" It is a tribute to Lloyd's abiding sense of humor and self-confidence that he immediately saw the humor in this practice and felt honored to be recognized in this unusual fashion.[6]

In its heyday the Dallas Civic Chorus was a model for community choruses around the country. They rehearsed faithfully every Tuesday night in Selecman Auditorium, part of SMU's Perkins School of Theology, and sang two to three performances per year. Their rehearsals were something of a sacrifice for their unsalaried conductor in that he rehearsed his SMU Choral Union from 7 to 8:15 p.m. on Tuesdays and then worked with the DCC from 8:30 to 10:30 p.m.! With typical Pfautsch reasoning, he commented that it was helpful to have the choirs rehearse on the same night, because once or twice they combined to sing with the Dallas Symphony. Selecman Auditorium was one of the few air-conditioned spaces in those early years and they felt lucky to be able to rehearse there. After the new arts facilities were completed, both choirs moved to the excellent choral rehearsal hall in the music building. The new space, designed by Pfautsch, was considered a model for future choral halls. Through the next several years many architects and conductors stopped by to examine the hall and ask Pfautsch about it.

The Civic Chorus' most widely acclaimed appearance each year was at the halftime of the Dallas Cowboys' Thanksgiving Day football game. They developed a tradition of singing "The Battle Hymn of the Republic" and doing it so well that CBS broadcast the entire live performance to millions of sports fans around the country. In 1970, the tenth anniversary for the chorus, Felix McKnight, editor of *The Dallas Times Herald*, wrote an editorial praising Pfautsch and the choir, now eighty members strong, for this stirring contribution to life in Dallas. He exclaimed that even the toughest grandstand quarterbacks would stand in awe and try to sing along with these inspiring performances. He concluded his paean with these words:

> It is one of the most unusual institutions in Dallas—this band of beautiful voices that breaks out two or three times a year in the brilliance of music. Not too many things are done these days simply to provide joy for others. The city of Dallas, the nation, should bow deeply in the direction of the Dallas Civic Chorus.[7]

Pfautsch was very proud of what the DCC accomplished. He regularly pointed out that this amateur group only practiced once a week and still achieved amazing results. In their early years, he performed many works with them, both sacred and secular, that otherwise would not have been heard in the city of Dallas. Many of their performances were, in fact, Dallas premieres. Harry Bowman wrote an article for *The Dallas Morning News* that claimed that of the sixty works performed by the DCC in the previous two decades, thirty-six were Dallas premieres![8] Among these were William Walton's *Belshazzar's Feast* and Leonard Bernstein's *Chichester Psalms* (the latter performed as soon as it was published). By the twentieth anniversary, in 1980, the choir had grown to ninety members. After the 20th Anniversary Concert in May, the chorus expressed their appreciation to the Pfautsches by giving him a Rolex watch and by giving Lloyd and Edie a substantial check to be used on an imminent trip to Europe. As usual the modest maestro was both surprised and overcome by the generous gifts.

Eventually, though, the musical scene changed in Dallas. A separate Dallas Symphony Chorus was formed and first appeared with the DSO under the baton of Eduardo Mata on September 23, 1977. Not only was there no possibility of the Civic Chorus singing for future symphony concerts, but the competing group drew some of the older group's members to it. Further, ironically due to the MSM program created by Pfautsch, there were many church choirs in the area with professional conductors offering programs and concerts that extended beyond their Sunday morning obligations. Then, too, many of the suburbs formed their own civic choruses (Duncanville, Plano, Richardson, Mesquite, Garland, *et al.*). In short, there was less of a need for a Dallas community chorus. Increasing numbers of choristers held jobs that required frequent travel away from Dallas and the group began having trouble with regular attendance, especially among the men. The conductor felt that he would no longer be able to offer the quality of performance his audiences had grown to expect. Further, it was about this time that he was dealing with a forthcoming surgery. Worry about that distracted him from any desire to continue fighting the odds with the Civic Chorus. He told the board that their final concert of the twenty-fifth year would have to be canceled. All of this led to a decision that the twenty-fifth anniversary year would be the last for the Dallas Civic Chorus. It had been a glorious run and they had made their mark many times over, but it was time to move on.

The Civic Chorus voted to give their significant library to SMU in appreciation for the use of rehearsal and performance spaces all of those years. It was a real boon to the SMU library, especially for the Choral Union, and remains the primary source for large choral works on the SMU campus. Since the SMU new music budget in 1985 for three choral ensembles was only $1500 per year, it was of great help to Pfautsch to retain the use of those scores. The group had fulfilled an artistic need in Dallas and provided an outlet for those desiring to sing great and challenging music in artistically satisfying performances. It nobly met those needs for two and a half decades. It remains an important part of Dallas' cultural heritage and artistic history.

Although he never taught voice at SMU, except to fill in for a colleague as needed, Pfautsch was considered a part of the voice faculty and invited to their departmental recitals and juries. His professional career and accomplishments were such that the other voice faculty could not fail to recognize him as a colleague. In the early years at SMU he sang on the voice faculty joint public recitals, a practice he later abandoned as he found he had no time for practicing and keeping his voice in shape. He still participated as recently as 1990, though, when he sang Heinrich Schuetz' "Fili mi, Absolon" accompanied by piano and trombone quartet.[9] He was quite intentional, however, about letting the students see that he and the voice faculty regarded each other as colleagues and not as antipathetic (as often happens in university music departments). He encouraged the other voice faculty to sit in on auditions for the solos in the choirs' concert repertoire and actively sought their advice before making his choices. While the faculty itself was not always amiable and collegial, they all seemed to respect and appreciate Lloyd Pfautsch. In that limited sense he was a catalyst for cooperation among his colleagues in the Voice Department.

Occasionally filling in for an absent voice faculty member helped Pfautsch form some definite opinions about voice teachers. He had mixed feelings about the use of artist-in-residence positions on the voice faculty. Good singers do not always make good teachers, he explained. He remembered taking over Mac Harrell's students one semester when the opera star became ill. He considered Harrell an idol. Pfautsch had heard him sing several times during his New York days. But he was shocked when he found that Harrell did not teach any of the basic techniques of singing. Those students who already had a solid technique when they came to his studio were greatly helped by the experience and coaching of Harrell. However, those who did not were not taught basics, such as breathing techniques, before being coached on the major roles for their vocal range.

Thomas Heywood, on the other hand, was an artist who really did know how to teach. Singers, especially tenors, would flock to him from all over the country. Pfautsch felt that he had a unique gift for pinpointing exactly what needed improvement to enlarge and refine the singing of those hoping for a career on the opera stage. Although he had never taught voice before he came to SMU and knew very little repertoire outside of those roles he had sung, Heywood learned quickly on the job, using his gift of helping fine singers realize their potential in amazing ways. He was greatly admired as a teacher and a musician.

Because he was ubiquitous in the SMU Music Department, Pfautsch was an effective force for change and improvement at his university. One example of Pfautsch's positive influence on music at SMU can be found in the hiring of Robert Anderson, one of his former students at Illinois Wesleyan. Anderson had just finished two years of study in Germany with Helmut Walcha. He was in the first year of his doctoral studies at Union Theological Seminary when Pfautsch convinced the deans of theology and music to hire Anderson for an open position in organ, music theory, music appreciation, and graduate organ literature. Anderson came to Dallas in February of 1960, met with the deans, and played an audition at Perkins Chapel for Dora Poteet Barclay, then head of the organ department and a well-known artist in her own right. Anderson remembered with a smile that afterwards Pfautsch took him to an SMU basketball game as a sort of treat. It was not, however, exactly Anderson's idea of a great reward. He summed up the experience as follows: "and that was the last basketball game I ever attended. After forty years here I still have never gone to another one!"[10]

Robert Anderson arrived in the fall of 1960, but by that time an unexpected event had arisen. It was discovered that Dora Poteet Barclay was terminally ill. She died the following March. So Anderson actually began his work at SMU by acting as head of organ studies with several adjuncts assisting with the applied organ studies while he taught the theory and appreciation courses. Somewhat like Pfautsch's position, Anderson's position involved supporting the MSM program, teaching in the music school, and serving as university organist and university chapel organist. After filling in for Barclay for one year Anderson was hired for her position. The second position in organ, theory and appreciation (Anderson's original position) was not filled. Pfautsch often stated, "I thought we were fortunate to get Bob then and I still think so today!"

It was the combination of Lloyd Pfautsch in choral music and Robert Anderson in organ that gave the MSM Program and music at SMU national prominence. Not only did they both enjoy national reputations, they also happened to work together very well. For several years Anderson accompanied the Chapel Choir while Pfautsch directed it. When asked how difficult it was for him to move from the teacher-pupil relationship with Pfautsch to that of teaching and performing colleague, Robert Anderson replied, "It was easy, because he made it easy for me." Although Pfautsch relinquished the Chapel Choir job after a few years, he and Anderson remained a formidable combination in the field of church music. They continued to collaborate on the annual Christmas services in Perkins Chapel until Pfautsch's retirement. Circumstances were such that in spite of their age difference, their retirements from university teaching were within a short time of each other. They left a legacy of fine graduates throughout the world, playing and conducting in important churches and schools both then and for many years to come.[11]

Pfautsch only held the position of director of the Graduate Program in Sacred Music for five years. In March of 1964 the Board of Trustees followed their master plan and established the School of the Arts at Southern Methodist University, combining the former School of Music and the departments of art, speech, and theater. Well-known playwright Kermit Hunter was hired as the first dean and Pfautsch was appointed associate dean and director of Choral Music. This was a trying time because the music faculty did not want to lose its separate identity and with it direct access to the central administration. Also, the other arts departments were leery of the larger music faculty and resented any funding they were awarded. However, the eight-million-dollar Owen Fine Arts center was in the process of construction and the plan was adopted.[12] Pfautsch also found this a trying time because he discovered two things he had not known before: (1) he resented the time that administrative duties took away from teaching, conducting, and composing and (2) working with Dean Hunter was very difficult and frustrating. In fact the experience convinced him to never again seek an administrative post beyond director of Choral Activities!

Relative to the first difficulty (time) is a recollection by Pfautsch of the day he was late walking into his Advanced Choral Conducting class because of a long-distance phone call he received in the ten-minute break after finishing a session of his Choral Techniques class. The call was related to his administrative duties. Since his office was next to the rehearsal hall the students knew he was there and waited for him. But, flustered by his tardiness he quickly grabbed his roll book and his lecture notebook and started class. He was congratulating himself on a reasonably smooth, if belated start and began discussing the "fricative r," when he sensed that the class was snickering and trying to hold back outright laughter. He finally stopped and said "O.K., What's so funny?" They sheepishly told him "you are reading from the notes for Choral Techniques, right where we left off 15 minutes ago!" At this point he realized that teaching a full load and administering the music department as well was just not working out. It was too much even for one of Pfautsch's fortitude and determination.

The second difficulty of serving as associate dean (working with Dean Hunter) had long-lasting effects. He recalled that Hunter would leave so many copious and unpleasant notes for him in his office that he actually dreaded coming back to the office after a day of teaching. He remembered one particularly blistering note left the day after the dedication of the new Aeolian-Skinner organ in Caruth Auditorium. The president's wife, Mrs. Tate, had arrived late and since the auditorium was packed she had to sit at the side in a folding chair. A keyboard player herself, Mrs. Tate had spoken with Pfautsch after the concert and told him that she was thrilled that so many people had come and that she did not mind in the least bit sitting in a temporary seat. Hunter, however, thought this showed a lack of planning on Pfautsch's part (never mind that no one knew of Mrs. Tate's intentions to attend the recital until she appeared). While the situation did not bother the president's wife, it deeply disturbed the dean of arts! Hunter's difficult behavior left such an indelible impression on Pfautsch that when he and his wife Edie moved into their new house in 1999 he had to ask his wife not to leave notes for him on the steps up to his home office. It brought back too many unpleasant memories of his stint as associate dean! Although he could laugh about it by that time, the painful memory lingered.

While he was largely an unhappy administrator during those years as associate dean, Pfautsch did accomplish several things. He was proud of the fact that he started the Piano Preparatory Department at SMU. It was based on a successful one he had observed at Illinois Wesleyan. The first hurdle was to convince the piano faculty of the need for and value of such a program. Eventually Louise Bianchi got excited about the idea and agreed to direct the first program. By this time word had gotten out into the Dallas community and greatly upset the Dallas chapter of the National Guild of Piano Teachers. So Pfautsch, Hunter, and Bianchi agreed to meet with them and explain what they had in mind. The Guild was afraid that SMU would try to gobble up all the good students in town and leave them without enough students to fill their studios. Pfautsch explained that the goal was to teach graduate pianists how to teach. They only needed enough students to provide a laboratory for the master teacher and the student teachers. Reluctantly the Guild backed off and the program was launched. As it grew it turned out to produce a profit for the music division and so the dean became even more of an advocate. It is still a very successful and fairly large program with national recognition. The fact that in 2003 the program's director was appointed chair *ad interim* of the music faculty, at the request of that faculty, suggests that the field is widely accepted by other musical scholars and performers as a valid and appropriate one.

Also among Pfautsch's successes as an associate dean was his championing the acquisition of several new pipe organs for the university. Robert Anderson would decide what was needed and Pfautsch would try and sell his ideas to President Willis Tate. It helped, of course, that Mrs. Tate was interested in organs and organ music. When Robert Anderson arrived at SMU there were only two organs on campus, a terrible specimen at McFarland Auditorium (where Dora Poteet Barclay taught all of her lessons) and an attractive, but smallish Aeolian-Skinner organ in Perkins Chapel. Tate questioned the need for a third instrument on the campus, but Pfautsch convinced him that with a growing organ department it was important to have a concert-size instrument in the arts facility itself. So Caruth Auditorium was remodeled to accommodate a beautiful and large Aeolian-Skinner organ. It was also among the earliest university auditoria to have adjustable baffles on the side walls to "tune" the room's acoustics according to the needs of various performers and ensembles.

Next came the plea for a studio organ for regular teaching use. Thus a room was modified to accommodate the Holtkamp studio organ. Finally, there was a push for some practice organs as the department was growing and the larger instruments were in auditoria that were too busy with other events to allow for practice time by the organ students. So some rooms not yet completed were redesigned to accommodate practice organs. Even then, Pfautsch wandered through the construction site one day and discovered that the architect had forgotten about the need for higher ceilings in the organ practice rooms. So he halted the contractors and immediately called the architect, who rectified the oversight.

Once the MSM program was off the ground (it started with just two students, but grew quickly) Pfautsch became full-time in the School of the Arts. This allowed him to assume an administrative role in music. Carlton (Sam) Young, an MSM graduate from Boston University, who studied at times at Union Theological Seminary as well, was hired to head the MSM program and, like Pfautsch, to do some teaching and conducting in both the School of the Arts and the School of Theology. The two musicians collaborated on various projects. For several years they shared the conducting of the Chapel Choir. During this era Pfautsch attempted to establish a commissioned anthem series similar to the very successful one he had pioneered at Illinois Wesleyan. Although Hope Publishing Company did agree to publish the SMU Chapel Choir Anthem Series from 1960 to 1984, it was not as widely embraced by the university as a whole and was limited to practical anthems for small choirs. Due to inadequate funding, about one-third of the anthems (nine of twenty-eight) were written by Pfautsch and most of the rest by his composer friends (Daniel Moe, Jane Marshall, Carlton Young, Natalie Sleeth, and others). The university chaplain's office provided some financial assistance with the project but it never achieved the prominence or the broad acceptance of the Illinois Wesleyan series.

In his administrative role, Pfautsch convinced Carlton Young to teach beginning conducting in the music department. At the time there was only one conducting teacher in music and his beginning class had thirty-six students. He happily turned over half of his class to Young. Because both Pfautsch and Young were gone from time to time for conferences and festivals throughout the country they were able to fill in for each other when on campus. They also collaborated, along with Robert Anderson, on the annual Christmas service in Perkins Chapel. Young would place the Seminary Singers in the back balcony and Pfautsch would put his University Choir in the chancel. Pfautsch even wrote some two-choir anthems (SATB and TTBB) to use as final numbers for these services. Several of these were published: "Watchman, Tell Us of the Night" (1967, Flammer); "Nativity Carol" (1968, Hope); "Love's Antiphon" (1970, Heritage); *et al.* As more and more women were admitted to seminary study the Seminary Singers eventually evolved from a TTBB choir into an SATB ensemble. After that the closing anthems for the Christmas services were for two mixed choirs. For example, in 1977 Lawson-Gould published "A Wondrous Mystery" for SATB/SATB choirs.

The annual Christmas service was a Lloyd Pfautsch invention. He started it in his second year at SMU, utilizing his Seminary Singers and building and painting the pew candleholders himself. It was loosely patterned after a similar service at Yale University. It was a natural extension to share the project with Young once he became the conductor of the Seminary Singers. Pfautsch contributed his University Choir. In 1992, as Pfautsch's retirement grew near, he received a letter from former theology school Dean Joseph Quillian that expressed the feelings of many members of the university and Dallas communities about the annual Christmas service:

> Lloyd, the Christmas Service is one of my warmest memories of Perkins, and always will be. In addition to the best music in town, that service had a very special mystique. I always looked forward to it for weeks and lived on its comfort and lift for months.[13]

Not all of Pfautsch's Christmas music was tied to the annual services in Perkins Chapel, however. In fact his most popular piece, *A Day for Dancing* (1969) was written for his University Chorale. It also employed the dance department, as choreography was intended to be a key part of each performance. Theatre students were used, too, especially for lighting and narration. The composer requested the simplest staging possible to allow the ideas in the texts to shine through.[14] When I asked him where he got the idea for this twenty-five-minute work he replied:

> I don't think I've ever told anybody this, including Edie. The idea for *A Day for Dancing* sort of came from having done the Britten *Ceremony of Carols*. I thought, you know, there ought to be another way of celebrating Christmas with instruments because the Britten is not long enough to fill a concert by itself. The first carol I thought of was "Today Will Be My Dancing Day." So I ended up with *A Day for Dancing*. In fact, we did the first performance with the dance department dancing to both the Britten and my piece. I told Susan Brailove, a senior editor at Oxford University Press (NY), about that performance and she said, "Oh you didn't!" And I said, "Yes, we did!" She said, "Mr. Britten would not have liked that." I said, "Oh, really?" And she said, "He did not want that piece danced to." And I thought "Well, there's no indication of that in the score!"[15]

Pfautsch intended that his Christmas work be accessible to performers and listeners alike. He felt the instrumental parts and the chorus parts could be done by a first-rate high school choir or by most university or church choirs and instrumentalists. Although he was criticized from time to time throughout his career for writing music that was difficult, such comments were never leveled at this work. Scored for flute, oboe, bassoon, and percussion, the work is delightfully simple and direct in portraying the birth of Christ through carol texts. Pfautsch found most of the carol texts in collections such as the *Oxford Book of Carols*. But as usual, he added some text of his own to tie the pieces (and the story) together. The work was a success from its onset; in fact it far outsold any of his other compositions.[16] As his publisher, Walter Gould said:

> It was very big. *A Day for Dancing* encompassed a number of elements. It was a very well done piece and, in a way, ahead of its time. Today you see so much music staged, but most of the time the staging has no relationship to the music. In this work everything was beautifully coordinated. It still gets a good number of sales and a good number of performances. It's the kind of piece that colleges and universities really love.[17]

A Day for Dancing has been performed all over the world. While Pfautsch was probably not the first to pair dance and chorus in American composition, he was certainly among the first champions of this combination. One performance that Pfautsch was especially pleased about was the one at 4 pm. on Christmas Eve of 1973 at St. Bartholomew's Episcopal Church in New York City. It was listed in

Final rehearsals for *A Day for Dancing*, SMU (1969) – singers, dancers, and instrumentalists.

their Christmas services advertisement in *The New York Times*, and so drew a lot of publicity for its composer.[18] He was at the performance and was quite pleased that one of the readers for the service was the famous news anchor Walter Kronkite, considered in his prime as "the most trusted man in the U.S."

One attempted performance of this piece created amusement for the composer as he reflected upon it. The work was scheduled for performance by the Civic Choral Society of Richmond, Virginia, in December of 1971. The planned venue was Sacred Heart Cathedral. However, the bishop, whose office had previously given permission for the event, happened to drop in on a rehearsal of the dancers, who were wearing only leotards during their practice session. He felt the dance was too suggestive and improper for a House of God and withdrew his permission, ignoring the explanation that the dancers would be more fully clothed in the actual performance! The presentation was moved to one of four other Richmond churches made available as the word got out about the banning. Meanwhile, the bishop's pronouncement generated publicity in Richmond, New York, and Dallas[19] as well as other places around the country. Lloyd wrote to Walter Gould "We are now a success! We have been banned in Richmond!"

In many performances this piece was a pioneering one, as Gould had pointed out. Many churches lifted their ban on dancing in worship because of this work. Among them are Highland Park Presbyterian Church in Dallas and several Baptist churches in the area.

Another positive response to *A Day for Dancing* came from its first performance at Wichita State University in Kansas. The president of the university was so taken by the performance there that afterwards he told the director of choral activities he wanted this work done every year! Naturally the choral director found this edict a little

Ex. 11 A Day for Dancing, 1969

too restrictive but did appreciate the warm reception for his performance. The composer, of course, admired the president's enthusiasm.

Pfautsch's other piece for choir and dancers, *Befana* (1976) is a fine piece, too, but it receives far fewer performances because the dancers have to be more skilled. The title character usually dances *en point*, for example. On the other hand the three kings can be walk-on parts for non-dancers. For a performance at the University of Utah the head of the dance department told Pfautsch that she used a football player for the white king, an African-American basketball player for the African king and an Asian student for the Eastern king. The work has usually been staged with rather elaborate costumes, but it can be done with simple leotards and rustic ponchos for the dancers. Its performances have mostly come from schools with very strong dance departments.

The Dallas Civic Chorus also collaborated with a dance troupe for a set of performances of Menotti's *The Unicorn and the Manicore*, at the Kalita Humphries Theatre in Dallas (1960). That was Pfautsch's only other brush with dance and chorus united. Pfautsch himself only wrote the two works for choir and dancers. When asked if he thought *A Day for Dancing* would last, he replied, "Yes, I do think that one will last."

Pfautsch believed that there was a close relationship between dancing to music and conducting music. However, he pointed out to his students that there is also an important difference between them. Both use the body to convey something to an audience or a choir. The big difference, though, is that music actuates the dancers (they make their movements to coordinate with the music) while conductors actuate the music itself. Conductors have to be slightly ahead of the sound or they will not conduct, but merely dance to the music. To cue a choir you have to be there ahead of them. To indicate a phrasing you have to be slightly ahead of the group or otherwise it is too late, it accomplishes nothing. There are conductors Pfautsch watched who caused him to wonder how in the world the choir could follow them. It is really through repetitious rehearsal, rather than leadership, that they succeed. The choir is dependent upon the conductor. The conductor must know what is necessary for the choir to produce the consonants and the vowels at the right time, rhythmically, dynamically, and in terms of duration, and provide direction ahead of the beat. One has to believe that before one can get up in front of a group and lead them successfully, according to Pfautsch.

Yet another Christmas work intended for the general public was *God With Us* (1962). Again, Pfautsch noted in the preface that he intended this work for the small church choir and amateur instrumentalists. In a 1962 review for *The School Musician*, choral composer, conductor, and critic Walter Rodby wrote: "The golden pen of Lloyd Pfautsch continues to please, challenge and satisfy his many admirers; and with his latest major opus, *GOD WITH US*, we ought to burn at least one Christmas candle for this exceptional American composer, conductor and educator." He concluded his review: "We suggest you ask your music dealer to order a copy for your own library. We're confident it will be a nice Christmas present for you, and a real gift for your audience when you perform it."

With Carlton Young on board at SMU to assume some of his former duties, and the MSM program on a firm footing, Pfautsch turned his energies to another great love, teaching choral conducting. He had been a one-man lobbyist for a graduate program in choral conducting. The music faculty was reluctant to start a graduate program in a discipline for which there was no undergraduate program. In his cajoling, but firmly insistent way, though, Pfautsch eventually beat down the opposition and established one of the first Master of

Choral Conducting programs in the US. He insisted that the students study orchestral conducting as well as choral and with the aid of orchestral conductor Paul Velucci, he won that point, too. Like the first year of the MSM program, he began with only two students but the demand quickly spread to five or six students. The professor soon realized that more than four was not workable. It was partly a matter of his available time and partly that of enough valid ensembles for the graduate students to conduct. As it was, some students in the Women's Chorus and the Mustang Chorale (the training choir for the University Choir) complained that they only worked with Pfautsch for one semester and had graduate students as conductors for the second semester. Pfautsch, of course, was there every week, but he was not taking charge in front of the students. Rather he was recording them from behind with his video camera.

Pfautsch rather quickly became a well-known teacher of conducting. He had worked out a very specific method and series of lesson plans for his students, revising them each year according to what worked and what did not, as well as what new problems were presented by each new group of students. One example is his description of his first conducting class for the new students each year. He would give the students his setting of *Puer nobis* first. The trick is to realize that most of the 3/4 measures are actually in 3/8 and must be conducted that way. Trying to do them in 3/4 will not work. The second piece for this opening class was usually a more difficult piece with multi-meters, which challenged some of them more than others. The final work, which he called his *piéce de resistance,* was Emma Lou Diemer's *From This Our Freedom*. Pfautsch found that its unmarked, but constantly changing meters (9/8, 11/8, 3/8, 3/8, 3/8, 3/8, 5/8 and the like) really challenged all of the students and let them know that this was to be an advanced graduate course where one could assume that the basics were already mastered.[20]

Lloyd Pfautsch credited the advent of the VCR and videotaping with revolutionizing the way conducting is taught. He looked back with a sigh at the amount of teaching he accomplished in his choral conducting classes at Illinois Wesleyan compared with what he could do at SMU once videotaping was a possibility. A pioneer in its use, Pfautsch made videotapes of all of his students' work on a regular basis and of many of his own performances as well. He long remembered one student whom he felt used up too much rehearsal time with talking to the choir. Although the student was a very good conductor and musician, he did not believe that he had a problem in spite of what Pfautsch and his fellow students told him. So Pfautsch taped one of his rehearsals with the Choral Union and used a stopwatch to time him. In the twenty-minute rehearsal he had talked about 9.5 minutes: nearly half of the time allotted! Finally the student was convinced that he had a problem.

The VCR was the tool to convince many students that what they were currently doing was not working. Hearing Pfautsch tell them or their classmates tell them was not always enough, but seeing it on the TV screen was. One example is found in Pfautsch's insistence that left-handed people should conduct left-handed. His point was that one should do what is the most natural and for left-handed people it is usually more natural to lead with the left hand and cue with the right. He first started thinking about this idea when singing under Arturo Toscinini. One day *Il Maestro* came to a three-hour rehearsal of the choir and orchestra with a severe case of bursitis in his right arm. He actually could not even lift his right arm. So he conducted the entire rehearsal with his left hand. It was just as beautiful and clear because Toscanini was ambidextrous. However, no one said, "I can't see your beat" or "I don't know what you want when you use that hand." So this caused Pfautsch to realize that left hand conducting can be perfectly viable, contrary to what was taught in most schools of music at the time (and to some extent today). He had left-handed conductors go on from SMU to receive DMA degrees in conducting, still using their left hand to lead. Further, there are many examples of successful left-handed conductors in institutions and churches throughout the Southwest. One outstanding example is his student, Donald Krehbiel of Dallas, whose Orpheus Chamber Singers is one of the premier choral groups in the region.

Pfautsch also made several videotapes for use in the pedagogy of conducting. Not long after he arrived at SMU, he did a series of six, half-hour tapes for the Georgia State Department of Education's "Teacher to Teacher" project. The invitation came from a former conducting student at the University of Illinois who was serving as the head of the Georgia State Board of Education. He described how his former student had arranged for a high school choir to serve as the demonstration ensemble for one tape. Although he had never worked with that choir before, Pfautsch got the idea to prove that one can often help a choir sing the right vowel sound at a crucial place in the score by mouthing the vowel while conducting. To do this he turned to the choir and mouthed several vowels one at a time and then had the choir sing back what they thought he was asking for each time. Fortunately, the choir came through with complete success and his point was proven. Pfautsch contended that mouthing the words is not normally a good idea; but helping form correct vowel sounds when needed, can be.

Ever a champion of new choral music, in 1974 Pfautsch convinced the Board of the Dallas Civic Chorus to award Emma Lou Diemer a commission to write an extended choral work for them. The result was *Choruses of Freedom.* The piece Pfautsch used as his test piece in conducting class came from that collection. When he told Ms. Diemer about this use of her work she was quite flattered, writing back "It must be 'fun' to conduct!"[21] In another letter dated March 2, 1978, she thanked Pfautsch for suggesting that she send this work to Lawson-Gould, seeking publication. They did, in fact, publish this movement and one other from *Choruses of Freedom* at the same time. She was even more grateful to Pfautsch for his assistance a second time.

Pfautsch was also a career-long champion of music for women's voices. When he moved to Texas, Pfautsch was invited to speak on music for women's voices at the annual Texas Music Educator's Association meeting, which happened to be in Dallas that year. This was an opportunity to continue his crusade to promote music for women's voices, a cause he had begun during his years at Illinois Wesleyan University. The planning committee put him in a small room at the convention center, thinking that this topic would not be a popular one. The usual prejudice against music for women's voices reared itself again! But Pfautsch used the women from his SMU choir to demonstrate and covered a lot of literature that was not well known to the attendees. He pointed out that nearly twice as many women as men audition for All-State Choirs and argued that therefore more music should be composed to encourage them. To his delight and the planners' chagrin, the audience was standing-room-only and even overflowed into the hallway! Afterward he said to the officers "Do you still think there is little interest in music for women's voices?" The speech was later published in the Sigma Alpha Iota journal, *PanPipes.*

One course created after the advent of the MM in Choral Conducting proved to be among Pfautsch's most successful and popular. That was the Advanced Choral Arranging Seminar. Not only was Pfautsch himself one of the best arrangers in the US but he developed a very successful method for teaching those skills to promising young graduate students. Often three or four students in a single class would get their work published directly from their polished class assignments. Pfautsch offered the new works to his publishers to get his students started in the profession. Of course he was blessed with some outstanding students; among them Jane Marshall, Natalie Sleeth, and Dede Duson are the most published. But there were scores of others as well.

Part of his technique was based on his experiences in composition class at Union Seminary with Harold Friedell and part, as was always the case with Pfautsch, was his own, original, step-by-step approach. Assignments were made and each session a certain number of students were slated to present their work for the class to sing and for the professor and the class to comment upon. The intention was to first point out the strengths and then make constructive suggestions for improvement. Usually this worked quite well. However, the instructor recalled one year in which two of the men in the class were very free and insensitive with their criticism of everyone else's work, but thought extremely highly of their own offerings. Finally the class had had enough of their caustic criticism and when it was the obnoxious duo's turn to present their arrangements, the class retaliated. "To a person, they leapt upon them like a lion on a catch!" They criticized everything they possibly could, verbally tearing the works to shreds. After class Pfautsch called one of the class leaders into his office and said, "The class intentionally ganged up on those two today, didn't you?" When he admitted that they had, the professor said "Good! I was wondering how long it would take you to do that. It will be a lot more effective coming from you than it would have been coming from me." For the rest of the semester he found the two offenders to be much more part of the class and amiable in their comments on other students' works. They also seemed to get an inkling that their work wasn't quite as great as they had presumed it to be. As Pfautsch said, "They became one with the class after that. No more of this holier than thou, happy to point out what you need to work on attitude. They had learned a lesson." One of the two has done very well and the professor was very proud of his work and his music ministry. The other student he never heard from again.

The relationship between Jane and Elbert Marshall and Lloyd and Edie Pfautsch was a strong one for over forty years. They first met when the Marshalls started singing in Pfautsch's Dallas Civic Chorus. As the friendship blossomed it was Pfautsch who suggested to Jane that she should come back to SMU and get a graduate degree in choral conducting. Her bachelor's degree was in music performance (organ). So in the mid-1960s she did just that. She credits Pfautsch with teaching her the basics of conducting. She still uses much of what he taught her, but has put her own labels on it and organized it and adapted it to her needs. "I think Lloyd excelled in clarity in his teaching, and in diction, too. Clarity of gesture was his hallmark . . . and there is nobody better at it than he. He was a fine choral arranging teacher, too." In fact, when Pfautsch talked about his choral arranging students he said, "Well, there was Jane, and then there was everyone else." Marshall continued to feel very close to the Pfautsches. She and Lloyd talked regularly on the phone about composition and conducting matters and mutual concerns over publishers and the like. Unlike Vaughan Williams and Holst, however, they did not exchange manuscripts and criticize each other's music. Marshall claims that once she was no longer a student at SMU, Pfautsch never again made any criticism of her work, but was always totally supportive of what she had done. She finds that "incredible." Like many of his associates, she also comments on the fact that "He was always a perfect gentleman." She found, as did Robert Anderson, that it was easy to change roles from student and teacher to colleagues because he made it easy for them. The Pfautsches and the Marshalls were also close to Carlton (Sam) and Marge Young. For many years the three couples celebrated together on their mutual wedding anniversary dates. As Sam Young observed: "Lloyd has a unique combination of German pietism combined with a populist approach to music-making."[22]

Pfautsch's own composition style became more eclectic in the 1970s, incorporating elements of Renaissance and Baroque polyphony, for instance. In 1973 he published the challenging but effective "*Omnis Spiritus Laudet Dominum.*" As his careful directions indicate, the refrain combines four textures for the four voice parts, rather like a neo-Renaissance chanson or madrigal. The bass sings the longest (slowest) version in chant style (ametrical), the tenor sings a chorale-like version, while the altos are given a melismatic line reminiscent of some Bach choruses (both of these in 4/4 meter), and the sopranos sing the shortest, dance-like setting in 6/8. The repeats are arranged so that a different voice part ends the refrain each time. Pfautsch stated that in performance it came out a bit differently every time. However, he tried to end the three voices such that the remaining one would not have to sing an entire repeat of its part by itself. The exception was that the basses sing their part alone once through to start the piece and most of it again at the end before the coda. His idea was to conduct each new part as it entered and then let them carry on by themselves until they had sung the requisite repeats. It would be impossible to conduct all four voices once they were all singing. Unfortunately, this fact baffled a lot of conductors who might have used the piece (including the great Howard Swann) and so it did not really sell very well. Once one understands that no conducting is the best conducting as soon as the refrain includes all four voices, then the work becomes relatively easy to manage. The verses are quite easy to conduct and allow the choir to sound good as TB or SA or SATB. ("That was intentional," Pfautsch said.) It is a fine work and deserves more performances than it has had to date. While a madrigal or chanson texture is evident in the refrain, the overall style is better thought of as neo-Baroque, with a Bach-like chorale and melismatic settings and the use of the refrain as a *ritornello*. The piece ends with a wonderful four-voice *fughetta*, followed by the final *ritornello* and the five-measure *coda*.

When asked about the clapping used in this and several other of his works (*e.g.*, "Christmas in the Straw") Pfatusch stated that he normally asked a few rhythmically competent choristers to do the clapping while the rest did the singing. This created a better chance for good ensemble production than if everyone clapped and sang. The exception to this practice is the anthem "Sing Praises" for which he usually asked everyone to sing and clap (see ex. 10 above). "*Omnis Spiritus Laudet Dominum*" firmly established Pfautsch as a master of polyphonic choral writing. He understood how to adapt Baroque techniques to the twentieth century and make them his own. He used the anthem at several high school choir festivals and with his University Chorale. But few other conductors have been willing to tackle it. As several of his MM Conducting students have observed from time to time, most of his music is not really hard for the choir *if* the conductor is prepared and knows how to handle it. This work certainly presents an extreme case in point.

In 1988 Pfautsch made his last commercial videotape. *Coming Alive: Choral Directing with Lloyd Pfautsch* was published by Augsburg Fortress Press. It is a demonstration tape, showing different techniques for improving choral sound: warm-ups, breath support, and diction. The tape runs forty minutes. It received a favorable mention in *Billboard Magazine*.[23] His demonstration choir was the SMU Mustang Chorale (his training choir) from that year.

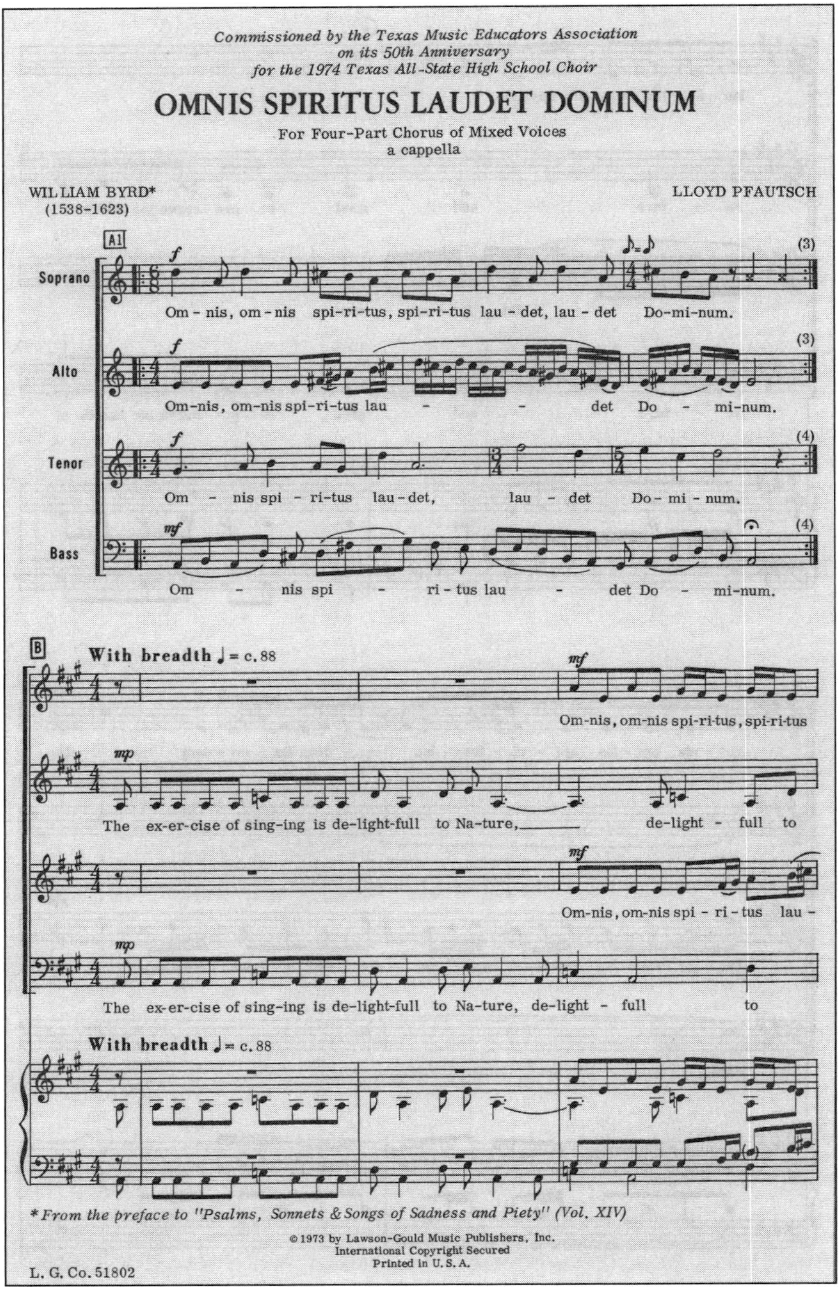

Ex. 12a Omnis Spiritus Laudet Dominum, 1973

PERFORMANCE DIRECTIONS

Section A is conceived as a refrain. At the beginning (A1) the bass line is sung first in its entirety and then repeated as indicated below and in the score. The tenors join at the first repeat of the basses while the altos join with the first tenor repeat and the sopranos with the first alto repeat. The manner of performance should be as follows:

Basses - Unhurried, like a Gregorian chant
(The bass line should be sung within 13 seconds and then repeated FOUR times before observing the fermata.)

Tenors - Sturdily, like a German chorale
(The tenor line should be sung within 8 seconds and then repeated FOUR times. The tenors enter at 14 seconds.)

Altos - With verve, as in J. S. Bach's *Magnificat* (Omnes generationes)
(The alto line should be sung within 8 seconds and then repeated THREE times. The altos enter at 23 seconds.)

Sopranos-Dancelike, as in a madrigal refrain
(The soprano line should be sung within 5 seconds and then repeated THREE times. The sopranos enter at 32 seconds.)

On each subsequent return to the refrain, ALL VOICES ENTER SIMULTANEOUSLY. The timing is as follows:

A2 - Sopranos repeat THREE times (15 seconds).
Altos repeat THREE times (24 seconds).
Tenors repeat FOUR times (32 seconds) and observe fermata.
Basses repeat TWO times (26 seconds).

A3 - Sopranos repeat FOUR times (20 seconds).
Altos repeat FOUR times (32 seconds) and observe fermata.
Tenors repeat THREE times (24 seconds).
Basses repeat TWO times (26 seconds).

A4 - Sopranos repeat SIX times (30 seconds).
Altos repeat FOUR times (32 seconds).
Tenors repeat FOUR times (32 seconds).
Basses repeat THREE times (39 seconds) and observe fermata.

The notation ✕ indicates a handclap.

Ex. 12b Performance Directions for Omnis Spiritus Laudet Dominum

Conducting was a very personal thing to Pfautsch. He stated that if five different conductors conduct the same group of amateurs the sound will be very different in each case. It will differ with professional singers or players, too, but in more subtle ways. In *Mental Warm-ups* he states that the choir will sing as its conductor conducts.

Pfautsch also thought that every choir should be allowed to find its own native sound. If the choir at a particular institution sounds the same year after year there is something wrong (for example the Christiansen tradition or the Westminster Choir College sound of the 1950s and '60s, especially). As personnel change, so should the sound of the choir. Otherwise, the conductor is just imposing his or her sound on them and there is a danger of the whole experience being reduced to an ego trip that can encourage bad singing. He wrote in *Mental Warm-ups*, p. 8: "A choral Conductor should operate like a highly successful salesman who concentrates on selling his product rather than selling himself."

Pfautsch believed that rehearsals should be the very essence of efficiency. He remembered one or two German conductors who came over to this country and had a hard time holding their American singers' interest. They were used to a very slow, methodical, repetitious, and overly simplistic approach to learning. Pfautsch, on the other hand, admired those who have a well-thought-out rehearsal plan and know how to help singers learn the notes quickly in order to get on to the business of making music as soon as possible. He urged his students to examine a piece of music and rate the various passages for degree of difficulty (from 1 to 5). He then started with the most difficult passage of the piece, no matter where it appeared in the work. Also for reasons of efficiency he advocated the use of the piano in rehearsal. He was sympathetic to the argument that the piano's temperament may not be ideal for singers, but in the early learning stages he found it indispensable to efficient learning. While he did a lot of *a cappella* rehearsing, the keyboard was there when needed to teach and to regain the pitch on tricky passages. Pfautsch had no patience for the European rehearsal style, which he referred to as "the slow method." He was much more attuned to Robert Shaw's philosophy: "I don't mind if there are mistakes the first time through, but I expect improvement the second time and by the third time I want to be ready to work on the music." While Shaw was referring to one of his professional groups at the time, he could normally maintain that same practice with his Collegiate Choral, an amateur choir in the sense of remuneration, but one in which most of the singers were trained musicians. Pfautsch had a similar situation in his university choirs (many voice majors and nearly all trained musicians) and he could expect rapid learning on a regular basis.

With most of his goals reached or well on the way at SMU, Pfautsch decided that he would finally take a one-semester research leave, the only sabbatical leave of his entire academic career! He arranged for Sam Young to teach some of his classes and paid out of his own pocket for another faculty person to take the rest of them. While such a practice was not common throughout the university at this time, it was the option open to him in the School of the Arts. The Pfautsches made a tour of England and Europe during their semester off, seeing the sights, meeting with many famous musicians, and attending a good number of inspiring concerts and worship services. Although they thoroughly enjoyed the sabbatical leave, Pfautsch never took another. One reason for that was the fierce loyalty he felt towards his choirs. He was reluctant to leave them in the hands of others, especially if the university was unwilling to bring in a competent visiting professor to cover his duties. The other reason was financial. Not only would he spend more money while on leave than when at home, but also Pfautsch was aware that he might miss many of the rather lucrative workshops, all-state choir and church festival appointments that he was accustomed to fulfilling on a regular basis. He quite frankly admitted that while his children were growing up and especially while they were in college he depended on these activities and on the royalties from his compositions to make ends meet. He was very much like an actor who is reluctant to turn down any valid role because he never knows when the next one might come along. Usually Pfautsch had as many or more offers than he could handle, but he never took that situation for granted. It is true that he cared deeply for his choirs, but it is also the case that he was what one could most charitably describe as frugal!

Lloyd Pfautsch in 1979: hairless top; hairy chin!

Chapter 5

The Dance of Adoration

(Popularity and Success)

AT THE SAME TIME HE was building two graduate degree programs at SMU, Lloyd Pfautsch was also building an impressive career throughout the United States as a choral conductor and a composer. From the late 1960s until his retirement in 1992 he was very much in demand to conduct All-State High School Honor Choirs and single and multi-church sacred music festivals (see Appendix G). As noted in the program for the 1977 National Convention of the American Choral Directors Association, by that stage he had been a guest lecturer at more than fifty colleges and universities.[1] Although he almost always included a few of his own compositions at these choral festivals, he seldom used more than one or two per festival unless those in charge specifically asked him to include more. Unlike some of his colleagues on the choral festival "circuit," Pfautsch was humble enough to feel that festival participants needed to experience a wide variety of good literature and did not use these occasions for self-aggrandizement. Nevertheless his anthems received enough exposure that they found a niche among the best church choirs (those conducted by well-trained musicians) and a majority of college and university choral ensembles in the United States. As Robert Anderson stated in an interview, "you could check the choral library of any church with a decent-sized choir and it would invariably include anthems by Lloyd."

Pfautsch often got rave reviews for his festival performances. He conducted the Sixth Annual Messiah Performance for the city of Wichita Falls, Texas, in 1958 and was so successful that he was invited back in 1959 to the seventh one as well. He also conducted a massed high school choir festival in Springfield, Illinois, in 1958. The reviewer noted: "The enthusiasm and spontaneity of these students for their task resulted in a program of high merit and interest. The singers . . . relished every direction Mr. Pfautsch gave them, judging from the tremendous ovation given him at the conclusion of the concert." The accompanist for that choir of 500, incidentally, was a high school student from Springfield named Marilyn Keiser. The reviewer praised her work as well. Dr. Keiser attended Illinois Wesleyan (after Pfautsch's tenure) and received both an MSM and a DSM from Union Theological Seminary. She is a world-renowned organist and Emerita Professor of Church Music at Indiana University.

In this era, Pfautsch also wrote books to express his ideas on conducting. These, too, helped to spread his reputation as one of the country's leading choral specialists. He published three books and a chapter in a fourth one, all of which are still in print in the new millennium! The first of these was *Mental Warm-ups for the Choral Director* (1969). Pfautsch said about this first effort:

> That was in a period of my life when I was sort of the angry young man. What I mean by that, I was concerned

about a lot of things that weren't happening in the choral field that I thought should happen. This was before the big push for a thorough education for choral conductors. It was still a carry-over from the thirties and forties, the "anybody-can-conduct-a-choir" attitude. And so I got the idea of putting together some famous aphorisms. I'd go to my boys' baseball games with my pad in hand and when I would think of something I would write it down. Quite frankly, I wish I could re-edit that. I wish I could excise a lot of statements that I made there, because some of them are a little too caustic. Although most of them I would probably stick by; for example, stating that most instrumental conductors do not understand singers, the technical demands placed on singers when they have to sing with an orchestra. Most of them could have profited from a three-hour in-depth session with Robert Shaw on how to work with a choral group. I also had some remarks about singers there, which I don't like anymore. But it was something I felt I had to do, and I wanted to vent my spleen—my choral spleen—so to speak, for whatever good it did anybody. It did me some good, getting those things off my chest.

Typical aphorisms from the book include the following samples:

On Conducting:

No amount of study of music literature, music theory, voice, etc. will ever supplant the importance of experience gained through participation in a vocal ensemble and through "standing in front of your own choir." Moral: all theory without practice makes jack a poor conductor.

A choral conductor, desiring more vocal intensity was once heard to shout, "*sing lustfully*!" Moral: all choral con-

> ductors are occasionally afflicted with "foot in mouth" disease, but it's rarely fatal!
>
> On Choral Contests:
>
> A choral contest is frequently an anathema. The conductor must receive a judgement *he* would rather avoid and the judge must make a judgement *he* would rather avoid. Usually the conductor thinks that he would make the better judge while the judge thinks that he would make the better conductor. How many times has neither been correct in his assumption?
>
> On Singing:
>
> We often tell our singers to "relax." But if you relax completely you will fall over! What we want to get rid of is *excessive* and *unnecessary* tension. Moral: ask and it might be given unto you. But know what you are asking for and why.
>
> Some voice teachers and conductors . . . stress affected production . . . and create a norm out of the affect. Thus, one hears some choirs who always sing with "an overemphasis on head resonance," while others always sing with a "smiling face." Right? Wrong! Wrong? Right!
>
> The many charlatans in vocal studios are usually the loudest in berating choral singing while protecting their own vocal "method." Moral: you can still fool some of the students much of the time.

Other choral directors and those trained in speech and drama regularly told Pfautsch after his choral concerts, "Gee, I could understand every word." One of his favorite comments from an audience member was "that's the best diction we have heard since Robert

Shaw was here a couple of years ago!" These kinds of comments were the motivation for writing his second book, *English Diction for the Singer* (1971). Richard Cox, in a review comparing them, mentions that Pfautsch's work is one of the three tomes universally regarded as the standard works on diction.[2] The first of these was Madeleine Marshall's *Singer's Manual of English Diction*. Marshall worked with both actors and singers as the diction coach for NBC and also at The Juilliard School and for its neighbor across 122nd Street, Union Theological Seminary. Marshall had personally coached Pfautsch when he narrated Honegger's *King David*. He had also used her book in his university teaching until he wrote his own. But he felt that Marshall geared her comments more to spoken English than to sung English. It is often what he regarded as stage diction, not singer's diction. This was especially true for her use of the schwa (the neutral or unaccented "e" sound: ə). He believed, for example, that the second and less important syllable of the word "father" should not be sung with the schwa (ə), as Marshall suggests, but rather with the "uh" sound (√) "fah-thuh." While this may seem a minor matter in speaking, it is far more important in singing, especially if the vowel in question is sung on a pitch of some duration.

Pfautsch got the idea for the drawings in his book from a Department of the Army film made with a World War II veteran who had lost his left cheek in battle. He had a cover for it and was viewed first as pronouncing all of the vowels and consonants with the cover on, looking quite normal. Then he was filmed with the cheek cover removed and one could see the placement of the tongue and shape of the mouth change as he pronounced everything a second time. A copy of this film was shown in Pfautsch's classes throughout his teaching career. Jane Marshall remembers that when she studied with Pfautsch he described it as "the film you would not want to go to lunch after viewing!" When Marshall was asked if she used Pfautsch's *English Diction for the Singer* she replied, "Oh yes, of course. It was published after my time as a student, but I still use it. While it is pretty clinical, he knows what he is doing with vowels and consonants and that I did not know about until I encountered Lloyd."[3]

Getting the book published was not an easy task. A renowned publisher, who shall remain nameless, approached him. However, he and the editor came to "sword points" over some of Pfautsch's comments that the editor wanted to change. Pfautsch felt the editor was wrong and so would not allow the changes. In frustration, he eventually talked to his friend Walter Gould about it. Gould agreed to publish the book, even though he had never before published anything other than music. Pfautsch drew the shapes he wanted for his examples and then got an artist at the SMU Print Shop to render them for him. Pfautsch wanted the drawings to appear on see-through plastic, but settled for thin paper. Plastic would have been cost-prohibitive for the little paperback. Nevertheless the author was grateful to Gould for publishing this, his first foray into the book-publishing world. It has done well through the years and still, in the twenty-first century, sells copies every year.

Abingdon Press requested the third literary effort, *Choral Therapy* (1994). They had started a series of small paperbacks on various aspects of church music. They wanted one for church choir directors who had very little background in choral directing. It is still true that in many churches, especially smaller ones, the attitude prevails that anyone who is accomplished in any aspect of music performance (singing, keyboard, or even string and wind instruments) is assumed to be capable of conducting a choir. Often these people want to direct the choir, even though they do not know enough to realize how ill-prepared they are. Certainly, Pfautsch points out, not every good singer is a good conductor.

Pfautsch viewed *Choral Therapy* as a "Reader's Digest" version of a more technical choral book. It was meant to offer guidance to choir directors throughout the country with limited background, outlining what they could do and what the choir needs. He also viewed it as a sequel to *Mental Warm-ups for the Choral Director.* He felt that conducting a choir, any choir, was a tremendous responsibility. Often the conductor is the only voice teacher an amateur singer will experience. As such, the "teacher" can either help or harm a voice, often with far-reaching consequences. This book was not as easy to write as Pfautsch had anticipated. He had to be careful to avoid the type of technical language he used in his university teaching, but still offer substantive guidance that was practical for the novice conductor.

In addition to his three books, Pfautsch also wrote the chapter on "The Choral Conductor and the Rehearsal" for *Choral Conducting: A Symposium* (1973), edited by Harold Decker, his successor after his one-year visiting position at the University of Illinois, and Julius Herford, his former mentor. He was one of five distinguished conductors chosen to participate in this venture. It has been a highly influential book and brought Pfautsch still further recognition. He modestly reminisced: "I really enjoyed doing that. That was a real challenge and I appreciated being asked to do that and join that nice, wonderful group of musicians. But people have told me many times and all over the country how much they felt they learned about rehearsals from the book."

The collaborative author enjoyed recalling an amusing incident relative to getting his chapter published in *Choral Conducting: A Symposium*. He sent the final draft to Decker, who in turn showed it to Herford. Decker wrote back to Pfautsch that Herford's only comment was that he felt too much time was spent on the use of humor in rehearsals. So Pfautsch replied to Decker's letter stating that he had actually pared down what he wanted to say about the importance of humor in rehearsal. Over the years he had increasingly found how important humor was in helping the pace of a rehearsal and in helping the interaction with the singers. He diplomatically concluded with: "Besides, in all the years that I have known Julius, going back to my student days at Union Seminary, it has been a source of great pleasure for me to see how he has used more and more humor in his lectures!"

The recalcitrant writer heard nothing further from his editors. But several years later his former student, Jan Harrington, spoke to him after Pfautsch delivered a speech for the Indiana Music Educators Convention in Indianapolis. Harrington had worked with Herford for both his master's and doctoral degrees at Indiana University. He told Pfautsch he happened to be having a lesson on analysis of some choral work with Herford in his study on the day after Pfautsch's letter to Decker had been forwarded to him. Herford told his pupil that he wanted to read him a portion of Pfautsch's letter. He proceeded to read the comments on his own use of humor in lectures. He stopped briefly, then looked up at Harrington and said: "Gee, you know, Jan . . . I am funny!" Those who knew Herford and his dry, Germanic sense of humor find his statement highly amusing.

Pfautsch liked the concept of the *Symposium* so much that once it was published he invited the other writers to Dallas for a live version of the book at Southern Methodist University. During the weeklong symposium, which attracted about eighty-five knowledgeable choral musicians from across the country, each author was asked to give a lecture on his chapter of the book. It was advertised as an opportunity for the authors to expand upon what they had written and for the conferees to ask questions. Various panels were devised to carry these discussions forward with questions from the audience and creative evening sessions were added to the week. At one, Howard Swann and Julius Herford discussed the interrelationship of their

A Choral Symposium, **SMU (1974): Julius Herford, Lloyd Pfautsch, Harold Decker.**

two chapters: "The Development of a Choral Instrument" and "The Choral Conductor's Preparation of the Musical Score." On another night Herford and Pfautsch were to collaborate. Herford spoke first on the responsibility of the conductor to study and analyze the score. He used the first movement of Brahms' *Ein Deutsches Requiem* for his examples. When he finished, Pfautsch started a smooth segue by pointing out that one of the most difficult challenges in the Brahms work is to bring in the chorus on "*Selig sind die toten.*" Pfautsch was claiming that good conducting could help the choir to enter properly. Herford somewhat gruffly interrupted: "That's not necessary, all you do is tell the choir to sing 'Selig sind' and they do it!" So Pfautsch thought quickly and replied: "Then to carry that to its logical conclusion all a keyboard person wanting to play Bach or Mozart would do is study the score and then sit down and perform it." "Oh, no, Lloyd, no" came the reply "you also have to have the technique." "Well that is what I am talking about! You have to have the proper conducting technique to help the choir sing well." It was difficult for the unassuming Pfautsch to take on his renowned mentor, but he felt it was crucial to his entire thesis that the importance of good choral conducting technique be recognized by all present. The symposium was an educational success. To have brought these distinguished writers to his home university was a real coup for Pfautsch. Once again his creativity helped to enhance his burgeoning career.

The ever-modest Pfautsch agreed with one of the critics of his literary style who wrote, "He is certainly not a gifted writer." But his motivation for producing each of his books was grounded in a consideration of the practical matters of the choral conducting art, not in any sense of a compelling need to express his creative urges through writing. Furthermore, in this writer's opinion the quality of writing rose higher with each new effort. There is no doubt that in his last two works he was easily capable of expressing his thoughts in a concise and useful way. His reviews also reflect a gradual acceptance of Pfautsch as a more than competent writer. Consequently these books have enjoyed wide interest and use. Walter Rodby, well-known choral director and composer, wrote a very favorable review of *English Diction for the Singer*. He describes Pfautsch in this manner:

> His interest and willingness to help others toward a higher excellence in the choral art has been demonstrated over and over again through his active participation in hundreds of festivals, clinics and workshops. Also, his

> publication productivity continues at a substantial pace, reflecting his sensitivity to what is needed and helpful for the average school and church choir director.

He continues with a discussion of the new book:

> In a word, this is a practical book, and we are confident that it will delight and illuminate choral directors all over the world. To be more explicit, we would say there is virtually no cloud-nine stuff in the book at all, but lots and lots of down-to-earth practical material which choral directors will be able to use at every rehearsal . . . both directors and choirs should benefit greatly from this comprehensive and well-written treatise.[4]

Rodby's opinions are typical of those Pfautsch encountered in his numerous travels throughout the country. So many people mentioned his books and asked questions about the parts they did not understand that it was clear that they were being read and are still influential in the world of choral conducting. He always relished these personal contacts and the opportunities they afforded to try and further explain any unanswered questions for his readers. He was always the first to explain that there is a good deal about conducting that can not be successfully written down. One has to demonstrate many concepts to teach them. His workshops and festivals became the vehicle for doing just that.

As his reputation grew, Pfautsch was one of the most sought-after conductors in the US for major festivals and symposia related to choral music. He recalled one important conference held at the Baptist seminary in New Orleans. Also on the conference roster and attending his lecture was none other than the revered composer, Randall Thompson. At a dinner at a Lake Pontchartrain restaurant one of the other conference faculty asked Thompson, "Who are some of your famous composition students?" He thought for a moment and then named about six, most of whom were fairly well known. On the way out to the car after dinner, however, Thompson suddenly stopped the little party in the middle of the parking lot, threw up his hands and said, "Oh, Lennie . . . how could I have forgotten Lennie?" All present knew exactly whom he meant (Leonard Bernstein).

In 1965 Pfautsch was engaged to conduct a choir of 2000 for the Convocation of Religion for World Peace held at the San Francisco Cow Palace on June 27, as described in the Prologue. The event was in connection with the twentieth anniversary of the United Nations and brought together leaders of seven of the world's largest religions with a common cause: world peace. There had been a similar gathering on the tenth anniversary (called the Festival of Faith) at which Robert Shaw had conducted.[5] Pfautsch always felt that Shaw had something to do with him being invited to conduct for this unique and momentous second convocation but that feeling was never confirmed. It is unclear how many attended this event, but Pfautsch remembers the hall as having been nearly full.[6]

The choir was so large and their schedules so diverse that Pfautsch had his first rehearsal with half of them on Friday in a big Jewish temple and with the other half on Saturday at a large church. Finally on Sunday they all got together in the Cow Palace. He found the varieties of robes, costumes, ethnicities, and races to be most inspiring. He loved the model of efficiency in dealing with these large numbers presented that day. He had the use of the Sixth Army Brass Band, playing what seemed to him "a block away and behind the choir" as well as Harold Mueller playing an Allen organ built for that locale and event. The music was chosen to represent all seven religions. The closing number was an arrangement for choir and brass of the hymn "Turn

Back, O Man." In the final verse when that choir sang "Earth shall be free and all her people one," the veteran choral conductor was nearly overcome with emotion! Because UN Secretary General U Thant both attended and spoke at the gathering, many of the UN delegates attended the service as well. Following the gala afternoon a dinner for "principal participants" was given at Trader Vics by co-chairs Dr. and Mrs. William Lister Rogers. Pfautsch attended this dinner.[7]

It was a huge success and Pfautsch received accolades for months after the event. In a letter following the event, George Low, music chair for the convocation, wrote that Archbishop O'Connor (who had delivered Pope Paul VI's message) left immediately following the final number to cable the pope with his excited and enthusiastic reactions. Low, who lauded Pfautsch's work, also mentioned that the recording of the afternoon program was being sent to all 115 member nations of the UN.[8]

While he was in San Francisco, Pfautsch also accepted an engagement to lecture at the Annual Convention of the California Choral Conductors Guild in the days preceding the UN Celebration and lectured at the University of Southern California (a sister Methodist school to Pfautsch's SMU) in Los Angeles in the week following. All told, it was a very successful trip and one that enhanced the status of his still-blossoming career.

During this era Pfautsch's compositions were often as popular as his workshops and festivals. One friendship that developed during this time and lasted until death, was with Jester Hairston, the prominent African-American composer and conductor. In reading Hairston's correspondence to the Pfautsch family, one gets a picture of an ever-closer relationship evolving, fed by mutual admiration and understanding. Whereas in 1969, Hairston's letters are signed "Sincerely yours, Jester Hairston," as early as 1970 they change to

"Sincerely yours, Jess," and soon after that they are merely signed "Jess." By the same token, his salutations move from "Dear Lloyd" to "Dear Brother Pfautsch" to "Dear Cousins" to "Dear Friends" or "Dear Lloyd and Edie." The language in these letters also supports the increasing warmth and understanding the two musicians felt for one another. Near the age of eighty-two in 1982 he writes, "You are so very faithful, Lloyd, I just love you and Edie down to yo' little toes." He goes on to mention that he had recently conducted a festival of his own music in the Mormon Tabernacle in Salt Lake City. He elaborates: "it was before an audience of 4100 people! I considered that one of the many highlights of 1982; especially knowing the past prejudice of the Mormons toward my race. But they have changed, thank God, and I love them for it!"[9] To commemorate his admiration and respect for Hairston, in 1969 Lloyd wrote one of his most popular anthems, "Go and Tell John," in the style of a spiritual and dedicated it to Hairston. He was rather apprehensive about sending a quasi-spiritual work to the acknowledged expert on this musical style, but, as was often the case, his fears were unwarranted. Hairston replied promptly and effusively expressed his approval and appreciation: "Your admiration and thoughtfulness in dedicating this precious spiritual to me is one of the greatest moments of my entire life. Thank you and thank you again is all I can say. And it is a hard job for me to keep from messing up this paper with tears. May God continue to go with you and inspire you to keep pouring out that great talent of yours." He continued in a somewhat lighter vein: "I have looked over this number and I'm sure it has to be a hit. Man! You're killing me with those 'soul' rhythms. Stay in your own back yard, Man!" He concluded his thanks with the ultimate compliment: "I will surely sell a lot of copies for you next winter. I intend to use it on my clinics all season."[10]

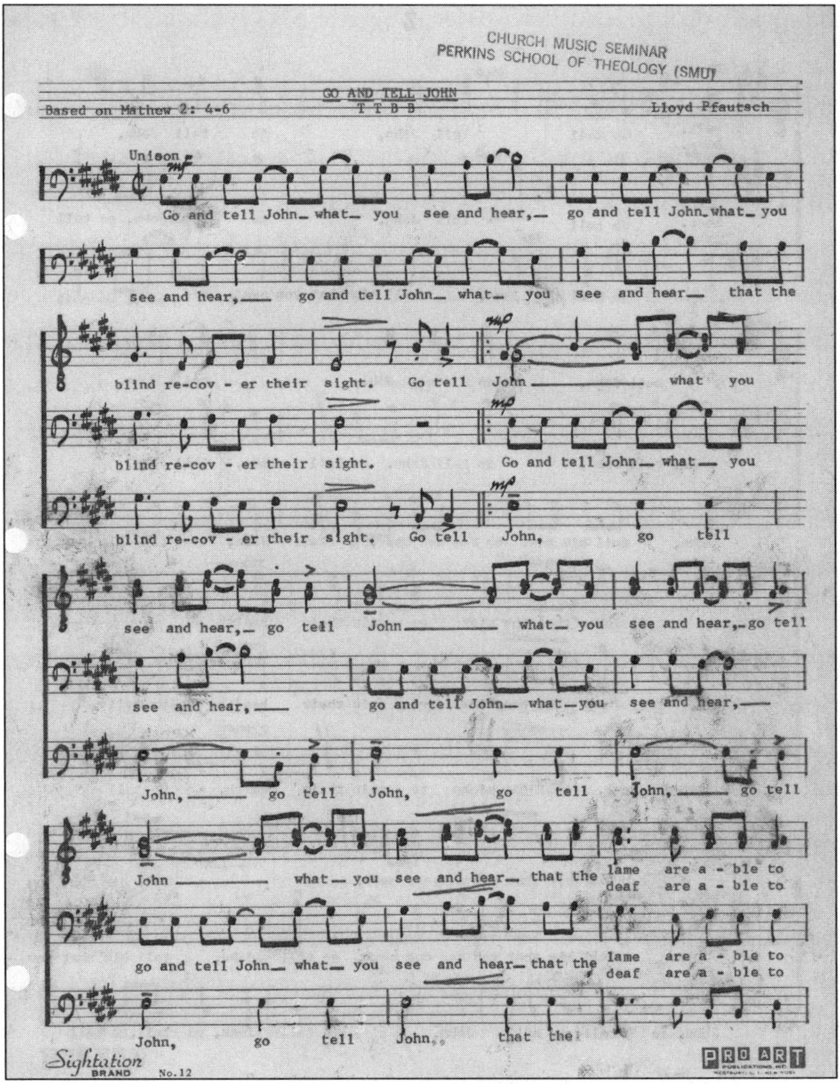

Ex. 13 Go and Tell John, 1969

Example 13 is Pfautsch's TTBB arrangement in his handwriting of his own anthem, "Go and Tell John." His men's choir arrangements were usually for the Seminary Singers group which, when he arrived on campus, had no female singers. He arranged this, and many, many of his other TTBB settings for SATB choir, either at the same time or soon after.

As early as 1956 Pfautsch had proven his skill at arranging spirituals with the haunting work "Witness." He did so again in 1957 with his arrangement of the spiritual version of Psalm 23 for children's choirs. In the same year he also published his arrangement of "Somebody's Knocking at Your Door." Then, too, in 1973 he arranged "I'm Free at Last." But "Go and Tell John" was a totally original work. Pfautsch had, in fact, captured the style of the spiritual so well that he nearly ended up in court over it! A composer in the northwestern part of the US was so certain that "Go and Tell John" was a spiritual handed down in the oral tradition that he boldly wrote his own arrangement of the text and tune and published it without getting anyone's permission or making any acknowledgements with regard to the source. It took a threat from Pfautsch's publishers and written opinions from Jester Hairston, Austin Lovelace, and Carlton Young to get the sales stopped and the existing copies destroyed. It was re-issued, however, with only a new cover to credit Pfaustch as the original composer. The insides were simply the old edition printed *in toto* with no added acknowledgement of Pfautsch. It appears the publisher chose to do the legal minimum at the lowest cost. In truth, the text and the tune of the first "Go and Tell John" were both original with Pfautsch. While it uses a biblically based text, Pfautsch is the one who created it. The authentic "sound" of the tune and the harmonization are one more indication of the superior ear possessed by this icon of choral music!

Soon after the success of "Go and Tell John" Pfautsch ventured into yet another musical style. He met the innovative worship team Richard Avery and Donald Marsh. He was attracted to the sincerity and simplicity of their message and their direct way of expressing it in worship. Pfautsch was moved to set two of their songs for SATB choir a cappella in 1970: "I Wonder Why?" and "Mary, Mary." The former was set for vocal solo as well and in still a third version for SATB/Organ (1972). In this writer's opinion these works exemplify the arranging talent and creativity that Pfautsch possessed in abundance. "I Wonder Why" was an interesting text set to a very mediocre tune in its original form. When the master arranger finished, however, it became a viable and dramatic piece of music and the tune was imbued with musical qualities well beyond those it originally held. Pfautsch had, indeed, created a "silk purse!" In 1972 he also set Avery and Marsh's "Here We Go A-Caroling" for SATB a cappella choir with finger cymbals and tambourine.

Another strong relationship with a prominent colleague developed during this era. Pfautsch built a friendship with the famous English hymn writer, Fred Pratt Green. Pfautsch was known for his ability to select important texts and then set them sensitively and appropriately. As with Hairston, the early letters from Green start with "Dear Professor Pfautsch" and close with "Yours sincerely, F. Pratt Green." After a couple of years, however, they switch to "Dear Lloyd" and are signed "As ever, Fred." Pfautsch set several of Green's hymns. The writer asked for tapes of the compositions as sung by Pfautsch's own choirs and was always obliged. His response to the taped performances is very positive. Among the successful settings of Green texts are "When in our music God is Glorified" and "Let Us Praise Creation's Lord." Several times Pfautsch asked to change a word or two and was given permission to do so. Green admired Pfautsch's ability to avoid gender exclusivity issues and still keep the integrity of the poetry he was setting.

Robert Shaw, ever loyal to Pfautsch, encountered him in Dallas several times through the years. They always found time to meet, even

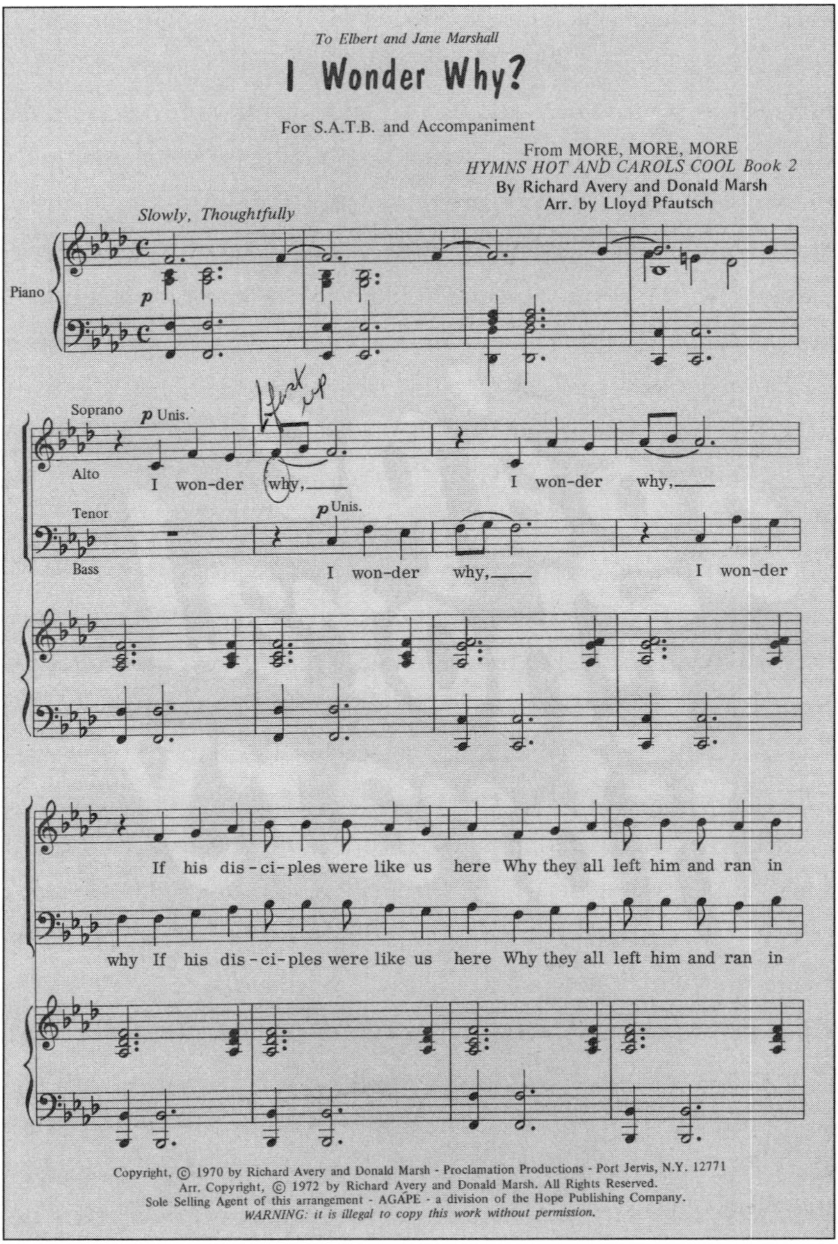

Ex. 14 Pfautsch arrangement of Avery and Marsh tune, 1972.

Ex. 15 Let us Praise Creation's Lord, 1987

with Shaw's incredibly busy schedule. Nearly every time Shaw also talked to or worked with Pfautsch's choirs at SMU. Pfautsch recalled one trip when Shaw was conducting the Dallas Symphony Orchestra and using the SMU Choral Union as the choir. They were performing Poulenc's *Gloria*, the Prologue to Boito's *Mephistopheles,* and Verdi's *Te Deum.* Pfautsch warned the choir that Shaw took singing very seriously. "He will expect you to be prepared, attentive and retentive. He can be either the nicest person you'd ever want to work with, or he can be very difficult. It mostly depends on what he hears from and sees in you. It's up to you to make this a pleasurable experience."

When he arrived, Shaw was very pleased with what he heard and saw. He spent some time polishing difficult passages, but also relaxed and spent some time telling stories to the choir. He told the singers that one time he was conducting Norman Dello Joio's *The Mystic Trumpeter* at New York's Town Hall. "You know how there are some people who just have to stand up and applaud the minute you finish?" he asked the choir. Yes, they certainly knew all about that. (The tradition for standing ovations at SMU is so common that one choir member asked Pfautsch if he could arrange a "sitting ovation"!) Shaw continued, "Well there was this middle-aged woman in furs sitting in the third row. As soon as I finished she stood up and starting shouting "Barvo, barvo, barvo!" That tale so amused the choristers that on opening night with the Dallas Symphony as Shaw took his first bow to the audience at the end of the concert he heard coming from the chorus behind him a thunderous chorus of "Barvo, barvo, barvo!" Shaw was so moved he could hardly keep a straight face to the audience. As he turned to the choir he burst out laughing loudly. The choir was so taken with Shaw that all 200 wanted his autograph on their programs. He looked around and said, "look, we'll be here all night if I do this. Let me get some programs from the Symphony management and I'll just sign them in my room at the hotel. We will hand them out tomorrow night before the performance." So the students settled for shaking his hand and left. True to his word, Shaw came to the performance hall the next night lugging two large Neiman-Marcus bags full of signed programs. According to Pfautsch the students were so impressed that they not only sang beautifully that night, but they never forgot their experience with Robert Shaw!

Upon his return to Atlanta, Shaw wrote the following letter to Pfautsch:

> Dear Lloyd:
>
> Youth concert week in Atlanta gives me a chance to catch up on correspondence and to study the Penderecki *Passion According to St. Luke*, which is imminent, and the combination of the two reminds me how pleasant an experience it was to work with your choruses at S.M.U. earlier in the season.
>
> They were handsomely disciplined and musically spirited, and I thank you most deeply for your work and theirs.
>
> Hope the Spring finds you and your family healthy and happy.
>
> Affectionately,
> /Bob/
> Robert Shaw[11]

Pfautsch recalled that sometimes Shaw's remarks were quite unpredictable. One time he was presenting at a church music workshop at San Francisco Theological Seminary the same week Shaw was conducting a festival at a big Roman Catholic church in town. Pfautsch went down to Shaw's rehearsal and at the break approached the podium. Shaw's opening remark was, "Well, Lloyd, I am not drinking anymore!" While he was stunned by the remark he was also aware that Shaw was very proud of his accomplishment. Both men credited his second wife, Caroline, with being the positive influence needed to help him shake that habit.

Shaw, according to Pfautsch, was very proud of all of his children, a trait he shared with Pfautsch. His son Thomas Lawson went to Yale's famous School of Drama and was very successful there. In fact, Shaw was there the night he died. He had gone to Yale to see his son in a play that was his senior acting/directing project. But after the performance the proud father had a massive stroke and died before the night was out. It is interesting that Pfautsch died from exactly the same cause (a massive stroke), although he was in such good physical condition that he remained alive but unconscious for a week before he died.

When asked if Shaw really did write letters to his choirs starting with "Dear People," Pfautsch said: "Yes, he did." They were written to his Collegiate Chorale after every rehearsal. One of Pfautsch's former master's students, Jerry Ullrick was singing with Shaw at the time the book *"Dear People"* came out in print. Ullrick asked Shaw to sign a copy as a surprise for Pfautsch. Pfautsch very proudly showed this writer the inscription:

> Dear Lloyd,
>
> I have been asked to sign this for you. And though I haven't read it, I'll stand by what it says on this page, and that's thanks for all you've done for our groups through the years and for choral music in America. So there! Bob[12]

Pfautsch was aware that Walter Gould tried to get Shaw to write a book on conducting. Shaw, however, could not see the point of it, or of giving that much time to such a project. Fortunately we do have his tapes of the rehearsals at Carnegie Hall, which are very instructive and inspiring. In contrast, Pfautsch, as discussed above, wrote extensively on the art of conducting.

A review of the correspondence saved by the composer-conductor reveals that Pfautsch communicated on a first-name basis with such contemporary musical luminaries as Anthony Milner, William Mathias, Knut Nystedt, John Rutter, David Willcocks, Renate and Heinz Werner Zimmermann, Emma Lou Diemer, and Malcolm Williamson, to name a few.[13]

In spite of being treated as an equal by so many prominent composers and other musicians, the modest Pfautsch only allowed people to call him a composer toward the end of his career. In fact, as recently as 1998 he was still not very comfortable with the epithet. When asked if he had ever been invited to McDowell House, as many less-recognized composers were, he replied: "No, I wasn't in that class." When this writer protested he continued, "No, seriously, Ken, seriously. They want people who write more than choral music." It is true that since McDowell was interested in piano and orchestral music that was probably a priority in their selection process. It is not true, however, that he was not in that class in terms of quality of composition. "When people called me a composer I would say I'm a choral conductor who wrote frequently for my instrument, the chorus." He next proclaimed, "I think a composer is one who writes in all media and does that as his primary profession." It was pointed out that early on his publications were more often arrangements rather than original works but later that was certainly not the case. He did admit that this was true. He also confessed, "Well, I suppose this was maybe partly an attempt on my part not to sound too grandiose or be guilty of self-aggrandizement. Or you might call it hypocritical, too, because I obviously like what I wrote and I performed what I wrote, too. And it was a pleasant experience to know that a lot of people wanted to perform the works. So I do feel like I did make a contribution to both the sacred and secular fields of choral music." "You still do," was the immediate response. "Well I was thinking this summer [1998] that on the basis of royalty returns they were not doing my music much any more, but my royalty return from Lawson-Gould this year was within $8 of what it was last year. So, you know, it's holding up. But some of the music with other publishers is not doing as well. Holt, though, has three of four pieces that are holding up real well, like 'I'll Praise My Maker' and 'Go and Tell John.'" "*Songs My Grossmama* has begun to tail off. But, golly, that goes back almost 50 years! Yet, there are some new conductors who are discovering it for the first time, which is satisfying, too." He continued: "I remember when Howard Swan told me how much fun he had doing it. And of course when I played it for Robert Shaw (to whom it is dedicated) he said 'I'm glad we have that in the catalog.'"[14]

Watching Pfautsch's own choir rehearsals proved to be most instructive for this writer. There in his "living laboratory" he put into practice all of the ideas in his books as well as others gained through experience. With his wealth of experience as a singer and as a conductor there were few problems he could not solve efficiently. He began with a short, but well thought-out and balanced set of warm-up exercises. First he activated the breathing mechanism and worked on uniform vowel sounds. He might start with the syllables *ho, ho, ho, ho* or *ha, ha, ha, ha*, making sure that everyone was singing the same vowel sound. He then added changes of pitch and range and finally other consonants such as *ma, ma* or *zing, zing*. He would end with syllabification of some direction or piece of information: *we, we, we, we, wih,wih, wih, wih, luh, luh, luh, luh, nah, nah, nah, nah, tuh, tuh, tuh, tuh, puh, puh, puh, puh, rac, rac, rac, rac, tiss, tiss, tiss, tiss, Frah, Frah, Frah, Frah, ih, ih, ih, ih, deh, deh, deh, deh, ee, ee, ee, ee*. ("We will not practice Friday.") Or if it was a Friday rehearsal and the school was playing a football game the next day, he would bark out, *Bee, bee, bee, bee, tuh, tuh, tuh, tuh, Bah, Bah, Bah, Bah, ee, ee, ee, ee, law, law, law, law.* (Beat Baylor!). The students would respond with "Yeah!" then keep right on singing. Warm-ups normally ended with *Bee, bee, bee, bee, see, see, see, see. teh, teh, teh, teh, duh, duh, duh, duh.* (Be seated.) But he would regularly change these messages enough that the choir had to pay attention and stay alert. He felt that if the same warm-ups were done in the same manner each time many singers would go onto automatic pilot and stop thinking about what they were doing and how they were doing it. He remembered with amusement that new choir members would take awhile to catch on to his messages. Some would find themselves the only ones left standing in their section for a time or two, but most caught on rather quickly. However, one of his finest bass singers (the kind with extra resonance where many of us have brains) was taking a conducting class in his junior year. When Pfautsch demonstrated this warm-up technique a big smile came over the face of the erstwhile bass who said, "Oh, that's why you do that at the end of warm-ups!" The professor replied in a shocked tone of voice: "John, you've been in choir for three years and you didn't know this? Then why did you sit down?" The response was: "Well, I saw other people sitting down." Naturally the class roared at the naïve response.

While he believed that it is important to start a rehearsal with warm-ups, Pfautsch also believed that you should not do the same ones everyday. Further, he did not believe in long warm-up sessions, especially when rehearsals were in the late afternoon and the students had been talking and singing all day long. He was a master at combining all of the important aspects of singing technique into a very compact set of warm-up exercises. For him it was a matter of pacing.

Pacing is, in fact, important throughout the rehearsal. Pfautsch said that he always tried to vacillate between greater and lesser intensities in the music being rehearsed. If he had a feeling that things were getting too intense, because he had been riding a section or the full choir too hard or for too long, he quickly shifted to an easier passage that allowed the singers to relax a bit. He added "I never say that's what I am going to do, I just do it. Because of the late afternoon time when I usually was working with the Chorale, I had to vary the intensity and style and approach a great deal to keep everyone alert and interested."

In reply to the question, "How do you teach melismatic passages in a chorus such as Handel's 'For unto us a child is born' to achieve clarity and precision?" the choirmaster offered these ideas: "First you have to recognize that with a choir of, say, 200 you will have a mass of sound to deal with. Further, many of them will have sung the work years ago in high school or college and will think that the way they did it then is the only way to do it." He used many devices, switching to new ones if the current one was not working well enough. One example was to have the choir sing the passage on *dah* or *tah* or even *kah*, which is hard to do but it does help to stabilize the eighth notes. If this did not work he might have the second row of singers just sing *bah, bah, bah, bah* while the others sing the words. This tends to keep the beat solid while allowing these singers to participate in the total sound. He would also have them separate the words. Another trick was to have the group (if small enough) walk around the room while singing the passage to solidify the rhythms in their minds. He greatly enjoyed working to solve problems like this, taking great comfort in the choir members' sense of pride and satisfaction in accomplishing a challenging task.

Another of Pfautsch's major theses was that it is necessary for the conductor to conduct good diction. He demonstrated that, by the use of subdivided beats, it is possible to indicate precisely where one wants a consonant or a vowel to happen. That and an insistence on uniformity of vowels were keys to his approach. One method was to have a quartet from the choir stand and sing "Since by man came death." He would find one singer whose vowel was farthest from the group's and then tell them to do it again but that the one singer must adjust her vowel only when he pointed at her. In this way the listeners heard the chord move into tune when the bad vowel was fixed. Yet another activity involved picking five men to stand and sing "Black is the color of my true love's hair." The first time sounded like five people singing at more or less the same time. Then he picked one singer and placed him in the center and asked him to sing it again. Next he picked the singer whose voice was most similar in timbre to the first man's and said "Now, you imitate him." The second man had to change his technique slightly to accomplish the mimicking. He did the same with the other three singers. Then they all tried to sing like the first man. Then he said, "now, forget the first man's sound and just work on getting the right vowel sounds." So he worked on each vowel in order until they were uniform. Finally they sang a seventh time, thinking only of the right vowel sounds. Invariably they reported that the last time felt the best and sounded the best. Not only had they learned the significance of uniform vowels, but also the dangers of trying to sound like any other singer, no matter how good the model may be. Pfautsch's favorite aphorism about diction was: "the more you work on diction, the less you will *have* to work on it."

One of Pfautsch's maxims in conducting was "Don't just borrow from or copy someone for the sake of borrowing or copying." He first learned that when observing Robert Shaw's conducting classes at The Juilliard School (see Chapter Two). He explained that "one must understand *why* the mentor is doing what she or he does and then you will be able to decide what will work for you and what won't." One of his favorite examples has to do with seating the choir. After choir directors learned that Robert Shaw seated his radio choir in quasi-quartet configuration they all wanted to do likewise, assuming that they would get the same great results. Having sung with Shaw, Pfautsch knew that the radio choir was seated that way because of the vagaries of broadcasting, not because quartet seating was any panacea for achieving good ensemble. Shaw had to avoid placing the louder voices near the microphone and also needed to eliminate blocks of sound coming from four different directions into the microphone. Finally, he was dealing with professional singers who were used to listening and using their voices to create the ensemble. In many, if not most, university and church choirs nothing of Shaw's situation exists. Consequently this idea cannot be blindly copied or it will be to the detriment of the choir. Pfautsch recalled one Christmas concert he attended at another Illinois university while on the Illinois Wesleyan faculty. The choir director, a friend, talked with Pfautsch afterwards and proudly said: "Did you notice that I had my choir sing in quartets?" His reply was "Yes!" But his thought was 'and I *heard* it, too!' She had placed a girl who had previously sung with Pfautsch on the end of the front row where her resonant voice stuck out on nearly every composition. Pfautsch's comment was "she should have been in the back of the center zone, or even on the top row." The point is not that one should never sing in quartets, but rather one should decide to do so for good reasons. Certainly the ability of the singers and the style of music performed are among the important considerations.

Pfautsch did believe in intentional seating plans, however. He firmly believed in using freshmen in his choirs, so that there never would be a time when there were not enough experienced singers to carry the group forward. He usually tried to place each freshman between two experienced upper class singers, if at all possible. One day one of his conducting students heard him explain his ideas on seating and said "Boy, do I know what you are talking about! When I was a freshman you placed me between two very good altos who were also excellent sight-readers. I had never been in that situation before. Both of these women were going ss-bb-kk-mm and ahh-ehh-ee, singing all of their vowels and consonants together. Before long I found myself doing it, too, without really trying." Pfautsch, in fact, counted on such osmosis to bring his new singers along more quickly and efficiently. He also habitually seated altos and tenors on his right and sopranos and basses on his left, normally with the men in the back. He kept the basses and sopranos on the same side of the choir because he usually got better intonation that way and having the altos and tenors (the inside voices) together gives one the flexibility of adding a tenor or two to the second alto part or an alto or two to the first tenor part, when the music or the choir personnel calls for it.

He was also careful to think of sightlines and blend when planning the seating. For example, if he had one or two very tall basses he put them in the next to the top row so that they would not stand out, and neither would their voices. He generally kept the high and low voices in each section together, especially if they were singing eight-part music. Some famous directors have each member of a section sing a phrase and then place singers according to which vocal timbres are the most compatible or the least strident together. Pfautsch did not use this approach. He believed that one gets homogeneity of sound through uniform vowel sounds. This then allowed the natural timbres of the singers to shine while singing the same colors to achieve the choral sound. For Pfautsch this method achieved the most exciting choral singing. It is akin to Roger Wagner's approach to the same subject. Wagner's flippant answer to the question of how to achieve blend within a section was "blend is boring!"[15] Another advantage to letting each member contribute to the timbre of the ensemble is that the rehearsals will be far less vocally taxing. Two hours of physical energy and concentration are bound to leave one physically tired, but it should not leave one's voice in a like condition. These are all reasons why Pfautsch regarded rehearsals as an ongoing process of choral development and choral education. Performances, he stated, "are merely reporting on what you have learned so far." After a performance one returns to the rehearsal experience the next day to continue the development process.

A man who practiced what he preached, Lloyd Pfautsch was renowned for the use of humor in his rehearsals. When this writer first attended one of his Chorale rehearsals at SMU he was introduced at the beginning of the rehearsal as a visiting conductor. The choir immediately responded, under their conductor's guidance, with a single clap of the hands. This greeting Pfautsch called "an applau"—the imagined singular form of the word "applause!" Although they must have done this often it still seemed to amuse the choir and it delighted this visitor.

Pfautsch admitted that he often planned a bit of humor at the beginning of rehearsals by intentionally messing up the listing of composers or compositions for that rehearsal on his blackboard. He found that students enjoyed it and that some of them even came early to make sure they could get the music in their folders in order from the clues given to them. Examples of these mislabels include "Vincent Copland" or "Aaron Persichetti" or "Johannes Vivaldi" or "Create in the beginning." He claimed with a disarming grin, "I thought they would find that more interesting than 22, 104, 76, etc." Following that same train of thought he also set unique times for his meetings and rehearsals, such as 8:29 a.m. or 4:02 p.m. He felt these were easier to remember than 8:30 a.m. or 4:00 p.m.[16]

On one occasion the maestro was trying to boost the morale of the basses before asking them to sing a challenging passage. He told them that his idea of heaven was him singing in a choir with 5,000 sopranos, 5,000 altos, 5,000 tenors, and only himself on bass. Then at a dramatic point in the anthem the heavenly choir director would stop the singing, look over at him and say, "a little quieter in the Bass section please, Lloyd!"

Once when the choir was on tour Pfautsch called them together before they went out to sing their first number. Naturally they were a little tense but Pfautsch eased the mood by telling the choir "Look, if you ever make a mistake in this concert, don't scowl like you are mad at yourself, just turn to the person next to you and glare at them as hard as you can!" It was reported that they all sang beautifully that night![17]

The students themselves also supplied some of the humor in his rehearsals. As one of his successful graduates, David Collett recalls:

> Throughout the year Lloyd would always name-drop famous persons whom he had encountered during his career, *e.g.*, Robert Shaw, Randall Thompson and the like. Somewhere along the way we decided that every time he dropped a name in rehearsal several of us would drop our keys on the floor. We assumed that LP was oblivious to this gesture as he was always so focused on the rehearsal. As students we had many hours of pleasure waiting for him to drop a name so we could drop our keys.
>
> But near the end of the year, when we were on tour with the SMU Chorale in Springfield, Missouri I learned differently. Just before we went on stage Dr. Pfautsch was reminding us of the importance of the city in which our concert was taking place. He reminded us again: "You know, Springfield was once the home of Abraham Lincoln." I reached into my pants pocket, preparing to drop my keys at the mention of Abe. Just then LP locked

> his gaze on me, pointed his finger and said: "Don't you do it, David!" I remember the shock when I realized that our supposedly unnoticed joke had been obvious to him all along.[18]

Typically Pfautsch enjoyed the humor of these student pranks. He was famous for his strong predilection for mentioning the name of his brother-in-law, Adolph Herseth, in his lectures and rehearsals. Herseth enjoyed a unique career of more than fifty years as the renowned principal trumpet of the Chicago Symphony. Pfautsch sheepishly recalled the time he gave a written final exam in one of his choral conducting classes. Every student managed to insert the name of Adolph Herseth into the answer on every question of the exam, some in very creative and amusing ways. For example, to a question such as "Discuss the use of the fricative *r*." One student wrote: "Well, Adolph Herseth always explained it this way . . . !" Afterwards he called them all in and said, "You guys and gals got together on this, didn't you?" They replied "Well, you referred to your brother-in-law so often during the semester that we thought we should refer to him, too, in our final exam!" Ever after Pfautsch found that quite amusing, but was only a little bit more careful with the frequency of his references to his famous brother-in-law. Some habits are too difficult to break, especially as one matures.

David Collett recalls that Lloyd's rehearsals were filled with intentional humor. Like many musicians he was hopelessly addicted to puns. He would shamelessly use puns and then gauge the attentiveness of his singers by the intensity and quickness of their groans! He remembers that one time the choir was sight-reading a new work and the tenor section completely missed their entrance. He stopped conducting and retorted to the erstwhile men: "that could have been a lot louder, tenors!"

Pfautsch himself liked to recall for his conducting classes the time he had a particular baritone in his choir. The student was a little older than his classmates were as he was an ex-G.I. He also studied voice privately with Pfautsch and they were on friendly terms. But the guy really liked to tell funny stories to anyone who would listen and sometimes they spilled out during rehearsal. One day Pfautsch was working with another section, but caught the baritone out of the corner of his eye as he was telling some story to his fellow baritones. The conductor wheeled around to say, "You know, Lenny, you really missed your calling. You should have been a Court Jester!" Not missing a beat, the singer could not refrain from retorting "You know, Mr. Pfautsch, I think you are a fool, too!" There was a collective audible gasp from the rest of the choir until Pfautsch began laughing, then everyone else broke into broad guffaws. Pfautsch's reason for telling this story to his conducting protégés was to make two points: (1) the best humor comes out of the moment in rehearsal and is spontaneous and (2) it was important that he took the jibe in the spirit in which it was offered. Had he not laughed and instead said something negative to the student it would have upset the choir and accomplished nothing good in the process. He and the choir knew the student meant it in a good-natured way and he accepted it for that. He is a man who never lost the ability to laugh at himself; it was to the end one of his endearing qualities.

Pfautsch was perfectly comfortable with his decades of baldness. In his office was a sign advising him: "Don't think of yourself as bald —think of others as hairy!"[19] Kenton Kravig-Williams, another former student, fondly remembers his first choir tour with the Meadows Chorale in the spring of 1986. The students referred to it as "The Dead Presidents Tour" because they visited the birthplaces of several former presidents as they traveled. They also decided at one stop that they were going to celebrate Pfautsch's upcoming sixty-fifth birthday a bit early by giving him a bright yellow giant comb with a curly handle about two feet long. This, of course, only called attention to the fact that by then Pfautsch had been bald for several decades. Predictably, Pfautsch loved the comb and the gesture it represented and showed it off to former students and other friends at each tour stop along the way. Kravig-Williams feels that Pfautsch had an uncommon ability to generate respect from his students while making each of them feel like they were his grandchildren and warmly regarded by the mature maestro.[20]

Pfautsch had a very successful "second" career conducting high school and church choral festivals and workshops. Not only did they help to acquaint the country with him and his choral publications, but they also provided a significant addition to his earning power throughout his career. At a time when Southern Methodist University paid most of its faculty and staff (with the exception of the football coaches!) a sub-standard salary, he welcomed this significant addition to his paycheck. As mentioned in the previous chapter, one of the reasons he avoided taking sabbatical leaves was financial. The combination of his SMU salary, his composition royalties, and his guest appearance fees provided well for his lively family of six. So conducting festivals at which some of his works were performed helped to tie all of these efforts together both musically and financially. The popular conductor also looked upon his guest appearances as a good recruiting tool for SMU. However, his administrative superiors at the university did not always understand it that way. It is true that many of the students who enrolled in his MM-Conducting degree program had originally worked with him when they were members of All-State Choirs during their high school years. A glance at

Appendix F will give one a sense of how many engagements Pfautsch accepted and how geographically widespread they were.

Lloyd Pfautsch received many honors during his career. He held three honorary doctorates: Doctor of Music from his alma mater, Elmhurst College (1959); Doctor of Humane Letters from Illinois Wesleyan University (1978); and Doctor of Humane Letters from West Virginia Wesleyan University (1985).[21] Although he appreciated them all he was especially grateful for the first one, partly because it was from his alma mater, but even more so because he felt his status in the SMU School of Music was significantly raised when he became "Dr. Pfautsch," even though the degrees were honorary, not earned. The diversity of the schools mentioned indicates the breadth of his influence and reputation throughout the country.

Awards from universities and colleges also included the Rotunda Award from SMU (1960, for outstanding faculty), the Alumni Merit Award from Elmhurst College (1971), the Meadows Distinguished Professor Award and the "M" Award (both from SMU and both in 1983–84.) The "M" award is the most highly coveted recognition bestowed upon SMU students, faculty, staff, and administrators. According to the plaque it is awarded for broad, continuous, and inspirational contributions of time and talents in order to make the university, and indeed the world, a better place for all of us to live. SMU also granted him the status of Professor Emeritus at his retirement in 1992. Additional awards included about forty ASCAP Awards for Contributions to American Music, the University Scholar/Teacher Award from the Board of Higher Education and Ministries of the United Methodist Church, and the Distinguished Choirmaster Award from the Texas Choral Directors Association.

True to his German heritage, the successful composer-teacher-conductor kept detailed journals of his participation in musical events, of the weddings he celebrated, and of the royalties on his many published compositions. Although Pfautsch had no interest in a traditional pastoral ministry and only preached one or two sermons in his career he did perform quite a few marriages for current and former students, mostly at SMU's Perkins Chapel.[22]

Pfautsch also produced lists of all of his choral compositions and other publications, students who earned doctoral degrees after gaining an MM in Conducting with him and the MM-Conducting graduates who did not pursue further degrees. Many of these lists can be found in the appendices to this text. They paint a clear picture of how influential and successful Pfautsch really was. They also provide an interesting chronicle of many of the major events in American choral music and key participants in them during the last half of the twentieth century. Few of his peers compiled as impressive a record and, unfortunately for historians, even fewer of them did such a fine job of recording their activities in careful detail. Pfautsch's penchant for preserving information made the preparation for this book so much easier and more pleasurable.

The Eternal Dance

An Epilogue

ALTHOUGH LLOYD PFAUTSCH WAS THE first to admit that he had led quite a wonderful life, he had his challenges, too. Among them health ranked fairly high. He was generally a very healthy person, robust and athletic. But in his fifties he developed a hyperthyroid condition. It began when he was conducting at the Presbyterian Montreat Conference in North Carolina. In fact the rumor mill among church musicians started the fortunately false idea that Pfautsch was dying from this illness. He was not, but it did make him feel like he was burning up! His doctor, who had had the condition himself and who had also been a high school chorister under Pfautsch at an All-State Festival, recommended against surgery. The patient was thankful for that. Instead, he was given an "atomic cocktail" of radioactive iodine. He was made to lie still on his back and to be sure not to swallow for about eight minutes (which seemed like eight hours to him). Gradually the swelling did subside in the next few weeks and when he was completely over it, in about six months, he found he could sing again nearly as well as he did when he was thirty. He was angry, though, with the rumor mongers for awhile after that.

The second serious illness came in the late 1980s. He had a trans-urethra resection to fix a prostate problem, but the more serious and long-lasting issue was the depression that followed. It is not uncommon for men to fall into depression after such an operation. The fear of cancer, whether based on fact or fantasy, is a very real one in such procedures. Further, one's manhood can be a concern. But Pfautsch was wise enough to realize that he was not going to be able to handle this depression on his own. He admitted himself to a local hospital for a short stay. There he got onto the right medicine, after several trial courses, and in a relatively short time was coping quite well again. This writer and others taught his courses and conducted his choirs for him for one semester. After that he returned to SMU and was able to go full steam ahead until his retirement.

After retirement, although he had several offers to do workshops and conduct festivals (even a very tempting one in Hawaii) he felt the loss of no longer going to the university every morning. This type of grieving process led to his second bout with depression, but this time he knew the signs and sought help even sooner. Again the medicines had to be given in trial courses until the right amount of the right drug was found. After a few months he was back on an even keel and ready to take on several conducting jobs and to compose quite actively. His recovery was permanent this time.

The final health concern and the one that brought about his retirement had to do with his eyesight. He suffered from macular degeneration, a progressively debilitating disease. This gradual loss of eyesight was also the reason that he had to quit composing shortly after his retirement. He otherwise was in good health and in good shape due to a daily regimen that included an early-morning hike through his Park Cities neighborhood. He was also very careful with his diet, only occasionally giving in to his greatest temptation: ice cream!

Lloyd Pfautsch's final years at SMU were a mixed blessing. While the choirs did well and he continued to receive accolades and honors and to maintain his lively career in composition, his efforts were beginning to wind down. He was approaching seventy years of age and though still capable had lost some of the drive and creativity that had made him so successful as a conductor and teacher. In a 1980 interview for *The Mustang*, an SMU magazine, Meadows School of the Arts Dean Gene Bonelli was quoted as praising Pfautsch: "There are certain people who put their stamp on an institution, leaving an indelible mark on it, and Lloyd Pfautsch is just such a person. I see him and SMU as being inextricably entwined." But just eleven years later Bonelli felt obliged to encourage Pfautsch to retire. There were many enjoyable events in that final year, but the celebrated teacher-composer-conductor left SMU with some bitterness about the way he was encouraged to retire. He felt that his decades of distinguished service to SMU should have resulted in a more amiable conclusion to his teaching career. In the last few years he received what was unheard of for him: a few negative comments from students on his end-of-semester course evaluations. Most faculty receive these occasionally and can usually put them in perspective. But this was a new experience for Pfautsch and one he would gladly have forgone. The vast majority of his evaluations were, of course, still very positive, but he took the negative ones quite seriously. Even though they hurt, however, he was characteristically able to joke about them and share (not hide) his feelings with his closest colleagues. Although it hurt him at the time, his dean and his department chair really did him a service by encouraging his retirement. He was able to go out with dignity while he was still popular with most of his choristers and while their concerts were still excellent musical presentations. Ever the gentleman and professional, he was quoted in SMU's *The Daily Campus* as saying:

> I don't think of this as retirement, but as moving on. I will continue to do what I have been doing, just not at SMU. I'm going to continue composing, arranging, conducting and directing choral workshops and clinics. I already have workshops scheduled for next year in California, Hawaii, Maryland and North Carolina.[1]

While he had reservations about his departure from SMU, he had no such doubts about his students. Between the MSM and the MM-Conducting degrees Pfautsch mentored over one hundred graduate students, thirty-four of whom went on to receive earned doctorates in music (see appendices H and I). A large majority of these graduates continued to keep in touch with their beloved teacher until his death. He quite regularly called to tell this writer where one of our mutual students was now working or what she or he had just conducted or accomplished. Like his mentor, Robert Shaw, he was 100 percent loyal to his former students and professional colleagues and his other friends. This, in part, explains why he remained so popular and admired even in retirement.

There was evidence of his loyalty and concern for others throughout his career. For example, the famous hymn-writer, theologian, and preacher Erik Routley wrote more than one letter thanking Pfautsch for helping him get his green card after his employment at Westminster Choir College in Princeton, New Jersey. The following excerpt from a 30 September 1975 letter to Pfautsch demonstrates both his appreciation and his colorful style of expression:

> I had hoped to write earlier to thank you for your assistance in rescuing my resident status here; however, I was told in Newark N.J. (a place which only very great sinners should be condemned to visit) that my visa having run out my standing in the USA is entirely illegal,

> and that I'd better wait until they've made up their minds, which they will tell us about, perhaps, if we're very good, in November. . . . Thank you again for the admirable music you sent to swell my Pfautsch Pfile. . . .

Pfautsch dedicated his 1971 cantata *Gloria* to Erik Routley. Routley's reply upon receiving a copy of it was in his typically effusive style: "I am delighted to have a score of the GLORIA. High time it was published! It's a splendid piece and I'm shamelessly proud of it."[2]

In the fall of 1991 the Master of Sacred Music faculty and students presented a "Festival of Psalms" at Perkins Chapel in honor of Pfautsch's career and pending retirement. The celebratory worship service was an appropriate setting for the presentation of a significant number of his works. The two organists on the SMU music faculty played two of his pieces for organ and brass and twelve of his sacred anthems were sung with twelve different students doing the conducting. Nine lectors read, including the deans of Meadows and Perkins Schools, a faculty member from each school, an alumna, and a current student. This writer gave the homily, a tribute to the life and work of Lloyd Pfautsch (see Appendix K).

In the spring of 1992, during commencement week, a banquet was sponsored by Pfautsch's "other" school, Meadows School of the Arts. The evening celebration was held in the ballroom of Umphrey Lee Hall on the SMU campus and drew a large crowd of current students, alumni, and current and former faculty. Representatives of each of these groups spoke and an alumni choir was formed for the occasion. It was a gala celebration and helped to ease the entrance into retirement. At commencement the following day, he was awarded the rank of Professor Emeritus and experienced his own "graduation."

Except for his eyesight Pfautsch was in good health and found creative ways to enjoy his retired status until his death. He continued composing until his death, slowed only by problems of eyesight. One fairly late example is the beautiful and very useful setting "Lord Jesus, Think on Me." He was gracious enough to dedicate it to this writer and his spouse. It is intended for Lent or general use. Pfautsch takes the simple and beautiful tune Southwell and sets it simply, subtly, and so effectively. It is hauntingly attractive and yet attainable by most church choirs.

Many of his compositions are still issued and even reissued by publishers and one can find his compositions among those performed by All-State Choirs around the United States each spring. He has had a lasting effect upon the choral world and, especially, upon American church music of the twentieth century. His legacy will continue for decades to come through his students, his music, and the thousands and thousands of people of all ages who enjoyed singing under his brilliant baton. He remains much loved and warmly remembered throughout the land. His "days of dancing" made an indelible impression upon all of us privileged to experience any part of them.

Lloyd Pfautsch died at 10:30 a.m. on Friday, October 3, 2003, at Baylor University Medical Center in Dallas.[3] He had suffered a massive stroke at home on Saturday, September 27 and never regained consciousness. To the end he remained a good friend and a good listener to those who needed one. He was ever the consummate "gentleman" and reliable confidant, not to mention beloved husband, father, and grandfather.

Two services were held to honor the memory of Lloyd Pfautsch. The first, on 7 October 2003, was at Preston Hollow Presbyterian Church in Dallas. Nearly all of the immediate family attended as well as many former colleagues and choristers from the North Texas area. A choir of Pfautsch choral alumni, with the Preston Hollow Presbyterian Church Choir as a base, sang "How Lovely Is Thy

Ex. 16 "Lord Jesus, Think on Me," 1996

Dwelling Place" from Brahms's *Requiem*, "He Watching Over Israel" from Mendelssohn's *Elijah,* and Pfautsch's own "Seek to Serve." They were under the direction of PHPC Minister of Music Terry Price, an SMU alumnus and former Pfautsch protégé. Donnie Ray Albert, one of Pfautsch's most famous former choristers, sang Schubert's *An die Musik*. Clergy included fellow SMU Emeriti Professors Victor Furnish and Neill McFarland as well as King of Glory Lutheran Pastor John Lee and PHPC minister Reverend Elizabeth McLean. The organists were Mary Preston (from Pfautsch's church, King of Glory Lutheran) and SMU alumna Annette Albrecht (organist for the host church, PHPC). Remembrances were given by several members of the family.

The second service was held on November 14, 2003, at Perkins Chapel on the SMU campus. Perkins School of Theology, host for the service, was represented by Dean William Lawrence, who presided, and C. Michael Hawn, who chaired the planning committee and led the congregation in a most effective final choral response (the final verse of "Wondrous Love"). Remembrances were given by this author and by long-time Pfautsch cohort and friend, Carlton ("Sam") Young. A large crowd of alumni from the Master of Sacred Music and the Master of Music in Choral Conducting programs comprised one choir to sing his "Prayer of Dedication" conducted by alumnus William Carroll now director of choral activities at the University of North Carolina-Greensboro and "I'll Praise My Maker" conducted by SMU alumna Dana Effler, minister of music at First United Methodist Church of Dallas. The select Meadows Chorale sang "Music, When Soft Voices Die" and "The Serenity Prayer." The excellent choir was led by their new conductor, Alfred Calabrese, formerly a doctoral student of Pfautsch's student, Jan Harrington, at the University of Indiana. Harrington was also in attendance at the service. At a dinner at the home of this author, held in September of 2003, Pfautsch had told Dr. Calabrese: "Why, you are my musical grandson!" Thus it was especially fitting to see and hear the legacy of Lloyd Pfautsch in such an outstanding musical performance by a student of his student. Clearly the Pfautsch legacy of excellence was continuing at SMU!

In 2006 the Fellowship of United Methodists in Music and Worship established an endowment to fund The Lloyd Pfautsch Memorial Anthem series of publications. The plan is to publish a new anthem every two years and have it premiered at the National Convocation of the Fellowship. This is just one more way in which Pfautsch's name continues to be associated with excellence in new sacred choral music.

Daughter Debbie Pfautsch ended her eloquent tribute to her father at the October memorial service noted above with the following words:

> I feel sad that Dad wasn't always sure that his music would continue to be appreciated. The rest of us know that the music came from his heart and will continue to touch the lives of many. It has the sound of his essence: a loving, generous, tender, humorous and fun-loving man.
>
> The heavenly choir now has a new leader, and it's time to get the diction right!

To that the rest of us can only add "Sing on, Lloyd!" Amen.

Appendix A

Pfautsch Family Tree

Joseph Pfautsch b. 3/14/1795	m. 2/10/87	Margaretha Hermann b. 1800
Johann Pfautsch b. 8/6/1838 (Meineck, Bavaria)	m. 12/25/1881	Emelie Preuss b. 12/31/1859 (Hermann, MO)
Walter Pfautsch b. 9/7/1884 (Hermann, MO)	m. 4/2/1919	Ouida Henselmeier b. 8/9/1892 (St. Louis, MO)
LLOYD PFAUTSCH b. 9/14/1921 (Washington, MO)	m. 9/7/46	EDITH HERSETH b. 12/01/1922 (Hitterldal, MN)

Deborah	Eric	Peter	Jonathan
b. 6/23/47	8/25/49	10/10/50	10/24/52
(New York, NY)	(Normal, IL)	(Normal, IL)	(Normal, IL)

Appendix B

Chronological List of Musical Events Involving Lloyd Pfautsch

'38—Played Contrabasse Viol in the National High School Orchestra, conducted by Vladimir Bakaleinikoff at Municipal Auditorium in St. Louis, 31 March. Played Moussorgsky's *Night on Bald Mountain*, among other works. 56 Vln, 15 Vla, 22 Celli, 13 KB, 16 Hrn, 9 Cl, 2 Bass Cl, 7 Fag, 6 Ob, 1 Picc, 10 Fl, 10 Trpt/Cornet, 9 Tromb, 1 B-flat Sousaphone, 3 Hrp, 5 Perc.

'46 —Sang *Elijah* at The Church of the Messiah in Patterson, NJ

'46 —Review of Shaw's Christmas Concert (Dec 23) at Carnegie Hall. Sang bass solo in Bach's Cantata No. 64 "*Sehet, welch' eine Leibe*" with Collegiate Chorale and Orchestra. Reviewed by Irving Kolodin in the *New York Sun*

'47 —Narrated *King David* at Carnegie Hall with Shaw conducting the Juilliard Chorus and Orchestra

'47 —Sang *Elijah* at HPMC in Dallas

'48 —Oratorio, *Israel at the Red Sea* (*Exodus 14–15*) performed in James Chapel, UTS on 12 May

'48 —Sang *Elijah* at Trinity Lutheran in Lancaster, PA

'51 —Taught at Union Theological Seminary, Summer Session

’52 —Sang *Messiah* solos at Bethany College (Lindsborg, KS) for the 70th Annual Performance in that city

’53 —Taught Summer Session at UTS

’54 —Sang *Elijah* at The Methodist Church of Berea, Ohio

’56 —Sang *Elijah* at The Methodist Church of Lakewood, Ohio

’56 —Gave conducting clinic at Indiana University

’57 – Clinician for annual church music workshop at Westminster Presbyterian Church of Dayton, OH

’58 —Taught at Northwestern University, Summer Session

’58 —Conducted 6th Annual Community *Messiah* in Wichita Falls, TX

’59 —Taught at Union Theological Seminary, Summer Session

’59 —Conducted Florida All-State Chorus in Tampa*

’59 —Awarded Doctor of Music degree from Elmhurst College

’59 —Ordained at E & R Church in Washington, MO

’60 —Organized Dallas Civic Chorus

’60 —Promoted to Professor at SMU

’60 —Sang *Elijah* at St. Luke’s Methodist Church in Houston, TX

’61 —Judged and Conducted at the Southern California Junior College Choral Festival in Santa Monica

’61 —Sang Voice Recital at Lovers Lane Methodist Church; Robert Anderson, accompanist

’61 —Conducted 9th Annual Community *Messiah* at Wichita Falls, TX

’62 —Conducted Arkansas All-State Chorus at Hot Springs*

’62 —Conducted Festival Chorus for NaFOMM in Nashville, TN

’62 —Conducted Choir for joint meeting of Dallas and Fort Worth Chapters of the American Guild of Organists in Arlington, TX

’62 —Conducted 1st National Church Music Workshop at TCU in Fort Worth, TX

’62 —Sang Voice Recital for Texas Annual Conference at First Methodist Church in Houston, TX

'63 —Conducted Iowa All-State Chorus in Des Moines*

'63 —Conducted Youth Choir for the Presbyterian Church Music Conference at Montreat, North Carolina

'63 —Conducted 4th Annual District 4, Baptist General Convention of Texas Music Workshop in Houston, Texas

'63 —Conducted Nebraska All-State Chorus in Kearny*

'63 —Conducted at U. of Wichita for Kansas Music Educators Workshop

'63 —Conducted Region 5, TMEA Choir in Houston, TX

'63 —Conducted Region 7, TMEA Choir in Corpus Christi, TX

'63 —Conducted SMU Choir on Cokesbury's "Hymn of the Month" Album

'64 —Conducted Arkansas All-State Choir in Hot Springs

'64 —Conducted Region 10, TMEA Choir in Arlington, TX

'64 —Conducted Choral Festival for Wichita Church Musicians Guild, KS

'64 —Conducted Chorus at the 8th Annual Church Music Conference at the U. of Puget Sound, Tacoma, WA

'64 —Appointed Associate Dean of the School of Fine Arts at SMU

'64 —Article in *Dallas Times Herald* for April 29 "Revised Methodist Hymnal called 'Greatest of Century,'" mentions "another new hymn by Lloyd Pfautsch" and quotes Bishop Gerald Kennedy as calling it "The greatest Protestant hymnal of the 20th Century."

'65 —Conducted Convocation of Religion for World Peace in San Francisco Cow Palace with message from U Thant, Secretary General of the UN. 20th Anniversary of the Founding of the UN celebrated by a massed choir of 2000 from 60 California Choirs

'65 —Clinician for the U. of Southern CA and the Los Angeles Choral Conductors Guild Summer Course in Choral Conducting

'65 —Conducted 2nd Annual Methodist Youth Choir Festival in Oklahoma City, OK

'65 —Conducted Texas Jr. College All-State Choir in San Antonio (280 voices)

'65 —Conducted TMEA Region 10 Chorus in Grand Prairie, TX

'65 —Conducted Tucson, Arizona All-City Chorus

’65 —Conducted Lincoln, Nebraska All-City Choruses (Jr. High and Sr. High)

’66 —Given the Rotunda Award as one of 12 Outstanding Faculty at SMU

’66 —Conducted the 37th Annual Fox Valley Music Festival in Aurora, Illinois, with 1100 choristers, 400 instrumentalists**

’67 —Conducted Colorado All-State Chorus of 323 singers from 101 schools

’68 —Conducted 19th Annual All-City Chorus of 500 singers, Dallas

’66 —Conducted the Dallas Civic Opera Chorus, which preceded and formed the nucleus for the Dallas Civic Chorus

’69 —Given his 9th ASCAP award. Article mentioned others so honored included W. H. Auden, Gian-Carlo Menotti, and Archibald MacLeish!

’70 —Dallas Civic Chorus sang at half-time of the Dallas Cowboys Thanksgiving Day game (70,000 in stands, millions watching on TV, according to a *Dallas Times Herald* article).

’71 —Given Alumni Merit Award from Elmhurst College (one of six given in their centennial year)

’72 —*A Day for Dancing* presented countless times and “banned in Richmond, Virginia.” Often the first dancing done in churches where it was given, including Europe and Australia.

’84 —Given the Meadows Foundation Distinguished Teacher Award

’84 —Given the “M” Award by SMU

’85 —Awarded the degree Doctor of Humane Letters by West Virginia Wesleyan University

’89 —Awarded an Endowed Residency at Anderson College in South Carolina

*Except for the early period, no All-State Choirs are listed because they appear in a separate listing found at Appendix G.

**After 1965 only highlights are recorded as all appearances would be too numerous to list.

Appendix C

A Lloyd Pfautsch Chronology

1921 —September 21 Lloyd Alvin Pfautsch is born to Walter and Ouida Pfautsch in Washington, Missouri

1930 —2nd Place in School Talent Competition (in Third Grade)

1931 —1st Place in School Talent Competition (in Fourth Grade)

1938 —Played Contra Bass Viol in the National High School Honor Orchestra (St. Louis)

1939 —Entered Elmhurst College (Illinois) as a pre-ministerial student

1939–42 —Directed choir at the Maywood (Illinois) Presbyterian Church

1941–42 —Elmhurst Men's Glee Club chosen Midwest winners in the Fred Waring Glee Club Contest and sang at Carnegie Hall; met Robert Shaw, who heard him sing a solo with the Glee Club

1942–43 —Directed choir at the Elmhurst E & R Church

1943 —Received a Bachelor of Arts degree from Elmhurst College. Begins Bachelor of Divinity degree at Union Theological Seminary in New York City

1943–46 —Bass Soloist at Brick Presbyterian Church (NYC)

1945 —Sang with Toscanini's NBC Chorus (P. J. Wilhousky, chorusmaster). Meets Edith Herseth, his future wife

1945–46 —Directed the High School Choir at Brick Presbyterian Church

1946 —Received Bachelor of Divinity degree, marries Edith Herseth and begins the Master of Sacred Music degree at Union Theological Seminary

1946–48 —Directed the choir at Manhassat Congregational Church, New York

1948 —Received Master of Sacred Music degree from Union Theological Seminary

1948–58 —Appointed Director of Choral Activities at Illinois Wesleyan University

1956–57 —Visiting Professor of Choral Music at the University of Illinois

1958–92 —Appointed to faculty of Southern Methodist University

1959 —Received honorary doctorate (DMus) from Elmhurst College

1961 —Received first of nearly 40 ASCAP Awards for contributions to American Music

1965 —Conducted choir of 2000 for the second Convocation of Religions for World Peace in San Francisco Cow Palace.

1966 —Received Rotunda Award for outstanding faculty, SMU

1970 —Dallas Civic Chorus sang at half-time of Dallas Cowboys Thanksgiving Day game

1971 —Alumni Merit Award (Elmhurst College)

1978 —Doctor of Humane Letters conferred by Illinois Wesleyan University

1983–84 —Meadows Distinguished Professor Award and the "M" Award, given by SMU

1985 —Granted Doctor of Humane Letters degree at West Virginia Wesleyan University

1991 —Distinguished Choirmaster Award given by Texas Choral Directors Association

1992 —Appointed Emeritus Professor of Music, SMU, upon retirement

1998 —Failing eyesight brought composition activity to a close

2003 —Died at Baylor Medical Center, Dallas October 3

Appendix D

Non-Choral Compositions by Lloyd Pfautsch

Vocal Solos

Puer Nobis for Mezzo, Piano (1947, Opus Five) Unpublished.

Three 13th Century French Songs for Mezzo and Piano (1949–53) I. Le Printemps (1949) II. Kalenda Maya (1949–52) III. Chanson de Chevalier (1953). French texts, unpublished.

Vocalize for Soprano and Piano (1951, unpublished)

"I Sing of a Maiden" for Soprano and Flute (1952, unpublished)

Two Songs for Voice and Violin on poems of Robert Nathan (1952) I. A Reflection II. Ethiopia (unpublished)

The Song of the Vineyard (*Isaiah 5:1–7*) for Baritone and Piano (1953, unpublished)

"The Poor Working Girl" a Folk-song Elaboration (vv. 2–4 added by the composer) Duet for Soprano and Alto (1953, unpublished)

The Virgin's Slumber Song for Mezzo and Piano (No date, unpublished) Arranged for Choir and Solo in 1967.

Solos for the Church Year (1957, High and Low) Lawson-Gould Collected and Edited by L. P. (no Pfautsch compositions included)

"Lutebook Lullaby" in *Contemporary American Songs*, edited by Bernard Taylor (1960, pp. 26–27) Summy-Birchard

Solos for the Church Soloist (1961, High and Low) Lawson-Gould Collected and Edited by L. P. (no Pfautsch compositions included)

"Birthday Wishes for the Christ Child" in *Art Songs by Contemporary Texas Composers* (1987, pp. 3–4) Southern Music Company

Six Songs by Lloyd Pfautsch (1991, High and Low) Lawson-Gould

Organ Music

"If Thou But Suffer God to Guide Thee" (1961) Robert King for Two Trumpets, Two Trombones and Organ

Three Organ Preludes on Hymn Tunes (1965) Augsburg Publishing. (Reassigned from Abingdon Press in 1988) I. Garden Hymn II. The Converted Thief III. Warrenton

Festival Prelude on "I'll Praise My Maker"(1967) Abingdon Press. Three Trumpets, Two Trombones and Organ (adaptation of the 1960 choral work)

Affirmation (1975) Carl Fischer. Organ, Percussion and Narrator (On a poem by Emily Brontë)

Brass Fanfare for *Ein' feste Burg* for Two Trumpets, Two Trombones and Organ and Congregation (no date, unpublished.)

Dialogue on *Ein' feste Burg* for Organ and Trumpet in C (1997, unpublished.)

Solo Flute

Dance Suite (no date, unpublished) I. Salterello II. Sarabande

Solo Piano

Dancetudes (1956, unpublished)

Books

Mental Warm-ups for the Choral Director (1969) Lawson-Gould No. 51474

English Diction For the Singer (1971) Lawson-Gould No. 51614

"The Choral Conductor and the Rehearsal," Part Two in *Choral Conducting: A Symposium*, edited by Decker and Herford (1973) Appleton-Century-Crofts

Choral Therapy (1994) Abingdon Press

Appendix E

Choral Compositions

1. The Resurrection [1948]
SATB S acap — unpublished

2. *St. Matthews Festival Mass* [1951] — unpublished

3. Sing in Excelsis Gloria! [1951] — C.C. Birchard 392
SATB/acap

4. *Five Narrative Carols* [1953] — C.C. Birchard 1616
SSA/Soli, fl, drum: I. Adam lay ybounden II. Coventry Carol III.Torches IV. O Little One Sweet V. Patapan

5. Kindergossip [1953] — unpublished
SSA/acap

6. Puer Nobis [1953] (written in 1947) — C.C. Birchard 1615
SATB/org or pno

7. Hello Girls [1954] folksong arr. — C.C. Birchard 1630
TB/pno

8. Three Craw [1954] folksong arr.. — C.C. Birchard 5251
TB/pno

9. What the Lord Requires [1954] — C.C. Birchard 2087
SA/org or pno

10. I Lift Mine Eyes [1955] — C.C. Birchard 2102
SA/org or pno

11. Noel, New Prince [1955] — unpublished
SSA/acap

12. The Ten Commandments [1955] U or SA/org or pno	C.C. Birchard 2084
13. Jimmie Nags Jeannie [1955] SATB/pno	C.C. Birchard 5050
14. How Far Is It to Bethlehem [1955] SATB/acap	Shawnee Press A-367
15. Easter Fanfare [1955] SATB/org or pno	M. Witmark 5-W3508
16. I Asked God [1955] SATB/org	unpublished
17. Spring [1956] SSAA/acap	M. Witmark 3-W3515
18. Youth Is the Season [1956]	unpublished
19. Thy Little Ones Are We [1956] carol arr.	Concordia 98-1140
20. *Songs Mein Grossmama Sang* [1956] SATB/pno	Lawson-Gould 562
21. *Songs Mein Grossmama Sang* [1956] SSAA/pno	Lawson-Gould 51020
22. Songs Mein Grossmama Sang [1956] TTBB/pno	Lawson-Gould 51021
23. Beautiful Yet Truthful [1956] folk song arr. SSA/pno	Lawson-Gould 549
24. Spring the Sweet Spring [1956] SSA/acap	Lawson-Gould 579
25. Luther's Joy Carol [1956] SA/pno or org	Summy-Birchard B-215
26. Hello! Mr. Schnibble [1956] SATB/pno	Shawnee Press
27. Man Is for the Woman Made [1956] SSA/acap	unpublished
28. Common Bill [1956] folk song arr. SSA/pno	C.C. Birchard 5200
29. Little Wheel a-Turnin' [1956] spiritual arr. SATB T solo/acap	Lawson-Gould 547

30. Rejoice in Bethlehem [1956] Lawson-Gould 621
SATB S solo/acap

31. O Lord, How Long [1956] R.D. Row 488
SATB/acap

32. I Ascend Unto My Father [1956] R.D. Row 6003
SATB/acap

33. Witness [1956] spiritual arr. Summy Publications 2243
SATB B solo/acap

34. Free at Last [1956] spiritual arr. Summy Publications 2251
SATB/acap

35. Thy Temple Stands to Serve [1957] unpublished
SATB/org

36. Rejoice in the Risen Lord [1957] Lawson-Gould 683
SATB/org or pno

37. Prayer of St. Francis [1957] Summy Publications 5066
SATB/org

38. The Lord is My Shepherd [1957] Summy-Birchard 5052
spiritual arr. SA/pno

39. Somebody's Knocking at Your Door [1957] Summy-Birchard 5157
Spiritual arr. SATB S & B soli/acap

40. A Riddle [1958] folksong arr. Shawnee Press
SATB/pno

41. The Oxen [1958] Shawnee Press
SATB S solo/acap.

42. When Christ Was Born [1958] Wynn Music 2201
SA/celesta

43. Balulalow [1958] Wynn Music 2202
SA/celesta

44. What Child Is This [1958] Wynn Music 2203
SA/celesta

45. Invocation [1958] Lawson-Gould 699
SATB/org or pno

46. A Time Carol [1958] Lawson-Gould 723
U/org or pno

47. Canticle to Peace [1958] SATB/band	Summy-Birchard 5218
48. To the Sunshine [1958] Schumann arr. SSA/pno	Summy-Birchard 5200
49. Brothers, Lift Your Voices [1958] TTBB/acap	H.W. Gray 2556
50. Sing Praise to God [1959] SATB/org	Summy-Birchard 5315
51. A Red, Red Rose [1959] Schumann, arr. TTBB/acap	Lawson-Gould 781
52. Music, When Soft Voices Die [1959] SATB S solo/acap	Lawson-Gould 793
53. Lamb of God [1959] Hassler, arr. SATB/acap	Lawson-Gould 800
54. A Hymn to the Him of True Love [1959] SSAA/acap	Lawson-Gould 816
55. Prayer and Chorale [1960] Mendelssohn arr. SATB/acap	Lawson-Gould 849
56. Know That the Lord Is God [1960] Handel arr. SATB/org	Lawson-Gould 872
57. Blessed Jesu [1960] Faure, arr. SATB/org orpno	Lawson-Gould 878
58. Agnus Dei [1960] Palestrina arr. SATB/acap	Lawson-Gould 884
59. Christ: Foundation, Head & Cornerstone [1960] SATB/2 trp & 2 trom or org	Lawson-Gould 959
60. God of Might We Praise Thy Name [1960] hymn arr SATB/3 trp, 3 trom & org	Abingdon APM-109
61. I'll Praise My Maker [1960] hymn arr SATB/3 trp, 3 trom & tuba	Abingdon APM-110
62. The Temptation of Christ [1961] SATB T & B soli/acap	Abingdon APM-142
63. Abraham and Isaac [1961] Capello ed. SATB T & B soli/org	Abingdon APM-143

64. Advent Carol [1961] Lawson-Gould 51014
TTBB T solo/acap

65. Easter Bell Carol [1961] Abingdon APM-168
Unison/Handbells

66. A Canticle of Commemoration [1962] Abingdon APM-224
SATB/acap

67. A Canticle of Commemoration [1962] Abingdon APM-225
TTBB/acap

68. Christian! Dost Thou See Them? [1962] Abingdon APM-226
hymn arr SATB/2 trp & 2 trom or org

69. *God With Us* [1962] cantata Abingdon APM-236
SATB S, T, A & B soli/org, timp, trp

70. Come, Thou Fount of Every Blessing [1962] Lawson-Gould 51074
folk hymn arr SATB/acap

71. Jerusalem, My Happy Home [1962] J. Fischer Bro. 9410
folk hymn arr SATB S solo/acap

72. Come, O Lord, Hear Now My Pleading [1962] Summy-Birchard 5515
Mendelssohn, ed SATB S solo/org

73. Psalm 150 [1962] H. Flammer 84725
SATB/trp

74. Fanfare for Christmas [1963] H. Flammer 84758
SATB/2 trp & 2 trom

75. Fanfare for Easter [1963] H. Flammer 84727
SATB/2 trp & 2 trom

76. Christ Is Arisen [1963] Schubert, ed. AbingdonAPM-274
SATB/acap

77. A Child's Prayer [1964] Chorister's Guild
Unison/hndbl

78. Reconciliation [1964] Abingdon APM-345
SATB (speaking)/trp

79. *Seven Words of Love* [1964] cantata Abingdon-364
SATB narrators/org

80. *Six Anthems for Junior Choir* [1964] Abingdon APM-368
U & SA/org or pno

81. I Thank You, God [1964] — Lawson-Gould 51215
SATB/acap

82. The Earth is Hushed in Silence [1964] — Broadman 454-014
U/org or pno

83. Fanfare for Christmas [1965] — H. Flammer 89204
SSAA/2 tr & 2 trom

84. Litany [1965] — Abingdon APM-420
SATB & children/org

85. *Grossvater's Historiker Versen* [1964] — Lawson-Gould 51208
SATB pno

86. Canticle of Thanksgiving [1965] — Abingdon APM-424
SATB/org & trp (or horn)

87. God So Loved the World [1965] — H. Flammer 84838
SATB/acap

88. A Canticle of Thanksgiving [1965] — Abingdon APM-424
SATB Narration/horn or trp

89. God Is My Strong Salvation [1965] — Abingdon APM-423
TTBB/acap

90. I Will Lift Up My Eyes [1965] — Abingdon APM-400
SATB/acap

91. I Want a Principle Within [1965] — Abingdon APM-399
SATB (2 parts) 1 trp & 2 trom

92. *Three Choruses on Norwegian Folksongs* [1966] — C.F. Peters 6866
Grieg ed & arr TTBB B Solo/acap

93. *Five German Folksongs* [1966] Brahms arr — Lawson-Gould 51235
TTBB/pno

94. On Hearing a Symphony of Beethoven [1966] — Lawson-Gould 51211
SSAA S Solo/pno

95. As on the Cross [1967] — Lawson-Gould 51299
SATB MS solo/acap

96. *Songs Mein Grossmama Sang* [1967] — Lawson-Gould 51319
SAB/pno

97. *Grossvater's Historiker Versen* [1967] — Lawson-Gould 51320
SAB/pno

98. Sing Praises [1967] — Lawson-Gould 51367
SATB/acap (handclapping)

99. The Gift Carol [1967] — Lawson-Gould 51348
arr. SATB/acap

100. The Virgin's Slumber Song [1967] — Lawson-Gould 51298
SATB A solo/acap

101. The Beatitudes [1967] — H. Flammer 84947
SATB/acap

102. Watchman, Tell Us of the Night [1967] — H. Flammer 84947
SATB-TTBB/acap

103. Knight without a Sword [1968] — Abingdon APM-694P
SATB/org

104. Joseph Dearest, Joseph Mine [1968] — Sacred Music Press S30
SATB/acap

105. The Lord Is My Light [1968] — Sacred Music Press S24
SATB S Solo/acap

106. Coverdale's Carol [1968] — Abingdon APM-421
TBB T Solo/acap

107. Nativity Carol [1968] — Hope 927
SATB/TTBB/acap

108. The Star Spangled Banner [1968] — Hope SP681
SATB/band or orch arr

109. Lord, Have Mercy [1968] Lotti, arr — Hope A 402
TBB/acap

110. Puer Nobis [1968] — Abingdon APM-422
SATB/org (re-issue from Summy-Birchard)

111. Musick's Empire [1969] — Lawson-Gould 51418
SATB/acap

112. Orpheus With His Lute [1969] — Lawson-Gould 51419
SATB S Solo/acap

113. Consecrate This Place and Day [1969] — Lawson-Gould 51420
SATB/acap

114. To Us Is Born Immanuel [1969] Praetorius arr — H. Flammer 85077
TTBB/acap

115. Sing to the Newborn King [1969] carol arr SATB/picc, 2 trp & drum	Lawson-Gould 51421
116. The New Is Old [1969] SATB S Solo/gtr, string bass & drums	Abingdon APM-855
117. *A Day for Dancing* [1969] Cantata SSATB/acap	Hope 3334
119. Love's Antiphon [1970] SSAA-TTBB/acap	Heritage Music H43
120. The Star Spangled Banner [1970] SSAA/acap	Somerset (Hope)680
121. Commitment [1970] SATB/vln	Augsburg 11-1596
122. *The Beatitude of John* [1970] Cantata SATB T solo/gtr, fing. cymb. & handbells	H. Flammer 4755
123. I Hear America Singing [1970] SATB/acap	Shawnee A-1092
124. Christmas in the Straw [1970] SATB/vln & handclapping	Lawson-Gould 51587
125. I Wonder Why [1970] Avery & Marsh arr SATB/acap	Hope A67104
126. Mary, Mary [1970] Avery & Marsh arr SATB Solo/acap	Abingdon APM-892
127. Join to Rejoice [1971] SATB/org (gtr)	Hope 3340
128. In Terra Pax [1971] SATB/acap	Lawson-Gould 51618
129. Jubilate Deo [1971] SATB/3 trp, 2 trom (or org) & cymbals	Lawson-Gould 51624
130. Gloria [1971] Cantata SATB A solo/3 trps & perc	Lawson-Gould 51552
131. Learn How to Sing [1971] SATB/orch (tr solo)	Carl Fischer 04869
132. Annunciation [1972] SSAA/harp or gtr	Lawson-Gould 51627

133. Go and Tell John [1972] TTBB/acap	Hope MM 9007
134. Go and Tell John [1972] SAB/acap	Hope CRY 3342
135. I Wonder Why? [1972] Avery & Marsh arr SATB/org	Agape AG 7104
136. Here We Go A-Caroling [1972] SATB/acap fing cym & tamb	Agape AG 7105
137. A Carol for Children [1972] SATB/acap, fing cymb, claves & woodblock	Heritage Music H 88
138. Praise the Lord Who Reigns Above [1972] SATB/acap	C. Fischer CM 7797
139. Prelude and Dance for Voices/Hands [1972] SATB/speech & body perc	C. Fischer CM 7803
140. This Is My Own, My Native Land [1972] SATB/band	C. Fischer CM 7887
141. He Rose! Hallelujah! [1973] SATB/trp	Hope 945
142. I'm Free at Last [1973] Spiritual arr SATB/acap	Somerset SP 714
143. Omnis Spiritus Laudet Dominum [1973] SSAA-TTBB/acap	Lawson-Gould 51802
144. The Guiding Christ, Our Shepherd [1973] SATB/3 trp & 3 trom	Abingdon APM-856
145. David's Lamentation [1974] SATB/acap	Lawson-Gould 51800
146. Go and Tell John [1974] SSA/acap	Hope Publ. Co. 3345
147. Hurry, Lord! Come Quickly [1975] SATB/org, gtr & str bass	Agape AG 7169
148. Prayer [1975] SATB/org	Lawson-Gould 51856
149. *Seven Affirmations* [1975] SATB/acap	Hinshaw HMC-114

150. The Lord Is in This Place [1975] — Abingdon APM-963
SATB/org, 2 trp & 2 trom

151. Witness [1975] (re-issue) Spiritual arr — Lawson-Gould 51900
SATB B Solo/acap

152. Lord, My God, Hear Now My Pleading [1976] — Hope A 479
Mendelssohn, ed SATB A Solo/org

153. Isaiah's Vision [1976] — Hinshaw HMC-142
SATB B Solo/acap

154. Laughing Song [1976] — Lawson-Gould 51949
SSAA/fl

155. Lovers Love the Spring (1976) — Neil A. Kjos GE 45
SACB/acap (in Cambiata Contempora)

156. His Spirit Leads On (1976) — Lawson-Gould 51972
SATB/2 trp & 2 trom or org

157. Blessed Is He Who Comes! [1976] — Hinshaw HMC-189
SATB/2 trp, 2 trom handbells & hand drum

158. *Befana* [1976] Cantata — Lawson-Gould 51966
SATB A Solo/fl, pic, ob, 2 trp, celesta, perc
(Dance)

159. A Wondrous Mystery [1977] — Lawson-Gould 52004
SATB-SATB/acap

160. Set Me as a Seal [1977] — Lawson-Gould 52029
SATB S solo/acap

161. Happy Is the Nation [1977] — Heritage H149
SATB/acap

162. Let Us Praise the Lord [1978] — Hope A-490
SATB/org, fl (or ob) & hand drum

163. Who Hath a Right to Sing [1978] — Lawson-Gould 52048
SSAA TTBB/acap

164. Be Careful What You Say [1978] — Lawson-Gould 52049
SATB/acap

165. A Litany for America [1978] — Lawson-Gould 52050
SATB/acap

166. The Oxen [1978] (re-issue) — Lawson-Gould 52061
SATB S solo/acap

167. What Sweeter Musick Can We Bring? [1978] — Lawson-Gould 52053
SATB/vln

168. Litany [1978] (re-issue) — Hope FS 957
SATB & Children/org

169. Christ Is the King [1979] — Agape LP 3710
SATB/org & hndbl

170. The Holy Son of God [1979] — Lawson-Gould 52089
SATB S & A soli/acap

171. In Music God Is Glorified [1979] — Hinshaw HMC-403
SATB/acap

172. Let Sounds of Joy Be Heard & — Lawson-Gould 52090
The Lotus Flower [1979] Schumann arr
TBB & TTBB/acap

173. The Minnesingers [1979] Schumann arr — Lawson-Gould 52091
TTBB/acap

174. Kyrie Eleison [1980] Schubert arr. — Agape LP 3711
SATB/pno or org

175. O Thou Who Camest From Above [1980] — Agape LP 3712
SATB/fl or ob

176. O Be Joyful in the Lord [1980] — Hinshaw HMC-445
SATB/2 trp & 2 trom or org

177. Requiem [1981] — Lawson-Gould 52167
SATB/chi or hndbl

178. *God With Us* [1981] Cantata re-issue — Lawson-Gould 52010
SATB S, A, T & B Soli/org, timp & trp

179. Hodie Christus Natus Est [1981] — Lawson-Gould 52209
SATB-SATB/acap

180. A Carol for Thanksgiving [1981] — Agape LP 3713
SATB/acap

181. The New Is Old [1982 re-issue] — Hope APM-855
SATB S solo/gtr, bass inst, & drums

182. God Is My Strong Salvation [1982 re-issue] — Hope APM-919
SATB/acap - hymn arr

183. Knight without a Sword [1982] — Hope APM-694
SATB/acap (re-issue of #103)

184. I Will Lift Up My Eyes [1982] — Hope APM-400
SATB/acap (re-issue of #84)

185. Easter Bell Carol [1982] — Hope APM-168
U/hndbl (re-issue of #59)

186. God of Might We Praise [1982] — Hope APM-109
SATB/org (re-issue of #60)

187. Mary, Mary [1982] Avery & Marsh arr — Hope APM-892
SATB S solo/acap (re-issue of #126)

188. Christian! Dost Thou See Them? — Hope APM-226
SATB/3 trp & 2 trom or org
(re-issue of #68)

189. Seasonal Songs [1982] — Lawson-Gould 52240
SATB/acap

190. The Ten Words [1982] — Augsburg-Fortress 3-8306
SATB/acap

191. I'll Praise My Maker [1982] — Hope APM-110
SATB/3 trp, 3 trom & tuba or org
(re-issue of #61)

192. Love Came Down at Christmas [1983] — Lawson-Gould 52278
SATB/acap

193. Seek to Serve [1983] — Hope APM-003
SATB/org

194. Eternal Grace [1984] — Hope APM-004
SATB/acap

195. Give God Glory [1984] — Sacred Music Press S-326
SATB/org & trp

196. Kyrie Eleison [1985] Dvorak ed. — Agape LP 3714
SATB/org or pno

197. Prayer of Dedication [1985] — Lawson-Gould 52360
SATB/org

198. Nativity Carol [1985] — Lawson-Gould 52359
SATB-SATB/acap

199. Echoes [1985] — Lawson-Gould 52372
SATB/acap

200. Winds [1985] SATB/acap	Lawson-Gould 52373
201. Stars [1985] SSAATTBB/acap	Lawson-Gould 52374
202. Visible Witness [1985] SATB/org or pno	Hinshaw HMC- 792
203. Puer Nobis [1985] SATB/org (re-issue of #3)	Lawson-Gould 52358
204. A Salute to Heritage [1985] SSAATTBB/acap	Lawson-Gould 52384
205. Psalm 43 [1986] Mendelssohn ed. SSAATTBB/acap	Hope APM-006
206. Instruments of Peace [1986] SATB/ob	Lawson-Gould 52385
207. He Is Coming [1986] SATB/2 trp	Lawson-Gould 52378
208. God Is Here [1986] SATB/hndbl	Augsburg-Fortress 11-2375
209. The Snow-White Messenger [1986] SATB/pno Folksong arr	New Music NM A-212
210. There is No Rose [1987] SATB/acap	Lawson-Gould 52404
211. Let Us Praise Creation's Lord [1987] SATB/2 trp & 2 trom or org	Hope M-3715
212. The Call [1987] SATB/org	Augsburg-Fortress 11-2389
213. The Golden Chain [1987] SATB/2 trp, 2 trom & org	Unpublished
214. Hello Girls [1988] Folksong arr SSA/pno	Lawson-Gould 52453
215. The Stewardship of Earth [1988] SATB/acap	Augsburg-Fortress 11-2452
216. The Seed of David [1989] SATB/acap	Lawson-Gould 52471

217. A Carol for Advent [1988] hymn arr SATB/org	Augsburg-Fortress 11-2494
218. A Carol for Palm Sunday [1988] SATB/acap	Augsburg-Fortress 11-2495
219. A Carol for Ascension [1988] SATB/acap	Augsburg-Fortress 11-2496
220. Sing Praise to God [1988] SATB/org (re-issue of #50)	Fred Bock Music BG 2037
221. Filled With the Spirit [1989] SATB/org	Lawson-Gould 52470
222. Advent Carol [1989] hymn arr SATB/acap	Lawson-Gould 52469
223. Hear Now My Prayer [1989] SATB T Solo/acap	Lawson-Gould 52498
224. Praise to the Lord [1990] SATB/org	Hope CY 3371
225. A Thousand Tongues to Sing [1990] SATB/2 trp & 2 trom	Hope CY 3372
226. The Caring Church [1990] SATB/org & trp	Unpublished
227. Saint Bridget [1990] SSAA/acap	Lawson-Gould 52538
228. Let Praises Ring [1990] SATB/acap	Unpublished
229. Three Challenges [1990] SATB/acap	Lawson-Gould 52537
230. A Carol of Commitment [1990] SATB/acap	Augsburg-Fortress 11-2519
231. The Temptation of Christ [1990] SATB T & B Soli/acap (re-issue of #52)	Lawson-Gould 52496
232. A Carol for Pentecost [1990] SATB/acap	Augsburg-Fortress 11-2550
233. The Birch Tree [1990] folksong arr SAB/pno	Lawson-Gould 52530

234. The Tabernacle of God [1990] SATB/2 trp & 2 trom or org	H. W. Gray GCMR 3589A
235. Two Blake Songs [1990] SSAA/acap	Lawson-Gould 52441
236. A Carol for Easter [1991] SATB/acap	Augsburg-Fortress 11-10016
237. A Carol for Epiphany [1991] SATB S solo/acap	Augsburg-Fortress 11-10014
238. Give Us Grace [1991] SATB/org	Augsburg-Fortress 11-552
239. Christ Loves the Church [1991] SATB/org	Unpublished
240. The Drummer and the Cook [1991] TB/pno Chanty arr	Oxford Univ. Press 95.117
241. A Carol of Thanksgiving [1991] SATB/org	Augsburg-Fortress 11-10022
242. *Israel at the Red Sea* [1991] Cantata SATB/T, B & S Soli/org, trp & tamb	Lawson-Gould 52520
243. Where Is Fancy Bred? [1992] SATB/acap	Lawson-Gould 52559
244. Kyrie Eleison [1992] Dvorak ed. SATB/org or pno (re-issue of #196)	Lawson-Gould 52610
245. The Gift Carol [1992] SSA/acap (arr of #99)	Lawson-Gould 52608
246. Keep My Commandments [1992] SATB/acap	Art Masters Studios 641
247. New Beginnings SATB/org	Unpublished
248. A Prayer for Singing Praises [1992] SATB/acap	Unpublished
249. Let Your Light Shine [1993] SATB Solo/acap	Hope A 669
250. Fancy [1993] SSA/2 trp & 2 trb or pno	Lawson-Gould 52640

251. He Will Give His Angels [1993] SSAATTBB/acap, Mendelssohn ed.	Lawson-Gould 52636
252. Knight without a Sword [1993] SATB/org (re-issue of #97 & #177)	Lawson-Gould 52667
253. Child of the Universe [1994] SATB/acap	Belwin Mills OCT2581
254. If You Are Risen With Christ [1994] SATB/3 trp, 3 trom & hndbl or org	Hope DFW 216
255. Love's Antiphon [1993] SSAA-TTBB/acap (re-issue of #119]	Roger Dean 15-047
256. The Snow White Messenger SATB/pno re-issue of #209)	Lawson-Gould 52641
257. Come, Holy Spirit [1991] SAB/org	Selah 405-611
258. Glory to God [1993] SATB/org	Unpublished
259. Isaiah's Vision [1993] SSA TBB-B solo/acap (re-issue of #153)	Lawson-Gould 52676
260. Life Has Many Rhythms [1993] SATB/org	Lawson-Gould 52676
261. The Temple of God [1993] 11-10217 SATB/org	Augsburg-Fortress
262. *Five Narrative Carols* [1993] SSA/fl, drum, soli (re-issue of #2)	Summy Birchard 45308
263. Wash Me Throughly [1994] Handel, ed & arr SATB/org	Lawson-Gould 52724
264. The House of God [1994] SATB/org	Selah 415-222
265. Consecrate This Place and Day [1994] TTBB/acap	Lawson-Gould 52730
266. The Threefold Truth [1994] SATB/org	Lawson-Gould 52727
267. The Devil's Nine Questions [1994] SATB/pno	Lawson-Gould 52768

268. Great Art Thou, O Lord [1994] SSATB/acap	Lawson-Gould 52756
269. My Heart [1994] TTBB/pno	Lawson-Gould 52750
270. My Younger Years [1994] TTBB/acap	Lawson-Gould 52751
271. My Native Land [1994] TTBB/pno	Lawson-Gould 52758
272. The Streets of Laredo [1995] TTBB/pno	Lawson-Gould 52794
273. Visible Witness [1955] SATB/org or pno (re-issue of #202)	Lawson-Gould 52560
274. A Day for Singing [1996] SATB/brass and/or org	Lawson-Gould 52788
275. Lord Jesus, Think on Me [1996] SATB S solo/acap	Abingdon 061881
276. Into Your Hands, O Lord [1996] SATB/acap	Lawson-Gould 52908
277. Enjoy Life and Sing [1996] SATB/acap	Hal Leonard 08505482
278. What Joy It Is to Worship Here [1997] SATB/org or pno	Lawson-Gould 52758
279. Sea Fever [1997] SATB/pno	Lawson-Gould 52919
280. Let Us Praise Creation's Lord [1997] SATB/2 trp & 2 trb, (or org)	Lawson-Gould 52879
281. The Lord Is My Light [1997] SATB S solo/acap (reprint of #105)	Abingdon 07135-6
282. Let Us Praise the Lord [1990] SSA/pno, fl (arr. of #162)	Santa Barbara 215
283. I Will Lift Up Mine Eyes (1998) SATB/acap (reprint of #84)	Abingdon 07320-0
284. This Is My Native Land SATB/pno (arr. of #271)	Lawson-Gould 52948

285. A Prayer for the Fleet [1999] SATB/acap — Unpublished

286. Let All the World Sing [1998] SATB/acap — Lawson-Gould 52948

287. We Will Praise the Lord [1998] SATB/pno — Kjos Music Co. 8873

*Miscellaneous Choral Works of Uncertain Origin**

1. Father, Forgive Them (c.1962) TTBB version of the First Word from No. 79
2. Hodie Christus Natus Est (c. 1964?) TTBB, 2 trpt., 2 trb version of No. 179
3. Songs of Praise the Angels Sang (c. 1964) TTBB
4. Gloria Patri (c. 1964?) SATB/TTBB Palestrina, arr.
5. Carol of Truth and Promise (c. 1964) TTBB (?)

*The above exist as photocopies of manuscripts in the composer's hand from the Perkins School of Theology Seminary Singers Library at Southern Methodist University. This writer has a copy of each and multiple copies are stored with the Church Music Institute of Dallas. Dr. Pfautsch only conducted the Seminary Singers for his first six years in Dallas, but continued to write Christmas music for them to perform with the Meadows Chorale, the premier SATB choir on campus, for many years after that at the well-known annual Christmas service of Lessons and Carols in Perkins Chapel. This explains why all of these, except no. 1 are settings of Christmas texts. The existence of No. 1 as a TTBB arrangement suggests that he may have done part of his Holy Week cantata, *Seven Words of Love*, with the Seminary Singers somewhat earlier than the 1964 SATB published version. This is the only TTBB movement extant.

Appendix F

Commissions

1. Spring (1956) | M. Witmark | SAI Chapter: IWU, Bloomington, IL

2. Youth Is the Season (1956) | Unpublished | SAI Chapter: IWU

3. Spring, the Sweet Spring (1956) | Lawson-Gould | SAI Chapter: IWU

4. Thy Temple Stands to Serve (1959) | Unpublished | St. Peter's E & R Church: Champaign, IL

5. I'll Praise My Maker (1959) | Abingdon/Hope | University Park UMC: Dallas, TX

6. Reconciliation (1964) | Abingdon/Hope | Highland Park Presbyterian: Dallas, TX

7. Musicks Empire (1968) | Lawson-Gould | State College of Arkansas: Conway, AR

8. Consecrate This Place and Day (1968) | Lawson-Gould | State College of Arkansas

9. Orpheus with His Lute (1968) | Lawson-Gould | State College of Arkansas

10. Christ: Foundation, Head & Cornerstone (1969) | Lawson-Gould | Community Church: Prospect Heights, IL

11. The Beatitude of John (1969) | Harold Flammer | Epworth Forest Choir School, OH

12. I Hear America Singing (1970) | Shawnee Press | Southern California Vocal Association

13. Join to Rejoice (1971) | Hope | SW Texas Youth Choir

14. In Terra Pax (1971) | Lawson-Gould | West Virginia Wesleyan College: Buckhannan

15. Jubilate Deo (1971) | Lawson-Gould | Elmhurst College Choir

16. Learn Now to Sing (1971) | Carl Fisher | Dallas Independent School District: TX

17. Praise the Lord Who Reigns Above (1972) | Carl Fisher | Furman University Concert Choir, SC

18. This is My Own, My Native Land (1972) | Carl Fisher | Air Force Cadet Choir, General R. J. Smith

19. Omnis spiritus laudet Dominum (1973) | Lawson-Gould | Texas Music Educator's Association

20. The Guiding Christ, Our Shepherd (1973) | Abingdon | Texas Conference UMC

21. High Flight (1976) | Unpublished | Air Force Cadet Choir

22. The Lord Is in This Place (1976) | Abingdon/Hope | Fellowship of United Methodist Musicians

23. Isaiah's Vision (1976) | Hinshaw | Mars Hill College, NC

24. Laughing Song (1976) | Lawson-Gould | Lyons Township HS:Western Springs, IL

25. His Spirit Leads On (1976) | Lawson-Gould | St. Peter's UCC: Elmhurst, IL

26. Blessed Is He Who Comes (1976) | Lawson-Gould | First UMC: Sherman, TX

27. Happy Is the Nation (1976) | Heritage Music | Westminster Presbyterian Church: Nashville, TN

28. Who Hath a Right to Sing? (1977) | Lawson-Gould | Illinois Wesleyan U. Collegiate Choir

29. Be Careful What You Say (1977) | Lawson-Gould | IWU Collegiate Choir

30. A Litany for America (1977) | Lawson-Gould | IWU Collegiate Choir

31. Christ is the King (1979) | Hope | Lover's Lane UMC: Dallas

32. Lord, As You Have Taught (1978) | Hymn Society | Hymn Society of America

33. O Be Joyful in the Lord (1979) | Hinshaw | Presbyterian College Choir: Clinton, SC

34. Requiem (1979) | Lawson-Gould | Midwestern University Choir: Wichita Falls, TX

35. A Carol of Thanksgiving (1980) | Hope | St. Paul's UMC: Syracuse, NY

36. Seek to Serve (1983) | Hope | Bellaire UMC: Bellaire, TX

37. Give God Glory (1983) | Sacred Music Press | First Presbyterian Church: Battle Creek, MI

38. Prayer of Dedication (1985) | Lawson-Gould | First UMC: Marietta, GA

39. Echoes (1985) | Lawson-Gould | Texas Choral Directors Association (TCDA)

40. Winds (1985) | Lawson-Gould | TCDA

41. Stars (1985) | Lawson-Gould | TCDA

42. Visible Witness (1985) | Hinshaw | St. Stephen's UMC: Mesquite, TX

43. A Salute to Heritage (1985) | Lawson-Gould | TX Music Educators Assn.

44. He Is Coming (1985) | Lawson-Gould | Fairbanks Choral Society: University of Alaska

45. God Is Here (1985) | Augsburg | First UMC: Midland, TX

46. Instruments of Peace (1986) | Lawson-Gould | Southern Illinois University: Edwardsville

47. The Call (1986) | Augsburg | First UMC: Pratt, KS

48. Let Us Praise Creation's Lord (1987) | Hope | West Virginia Wesleyan College: Buckhannan

49. The Golden Chain (1987) | Unpublished | First UMC: Roswell, NM

50. A Carol for Palm Sunday (1987) | Augsburg | Christ Lutheran Church: Tacoma, WA

51. The Stewardship of Earth (1988) | Augsburg | First UMC: Bartlesville, OK

52. A Carol for Advent (1989) | Augsburg | Westpark United Church of Christ: Cleveland, OH

53. Filled with the Spirit (1989) | Lawson-Gould | 2nd Presbyterian Church: Bloomington, IL

54. Hear Now My Prayer (1989) | Lawson-Gould | Congregational Church: Western Springs, IL

55. Praise to the Lord (1990) | Hope | Munsey Memorial UMC: Johnson City, TN

56. A Thousand Tongues to Sing (1990) | Hope | Wesley Memorial UMC: Washington, DC

57. The Caring Church (1990) | Unpublished | Bethany UMC: Houston

58. St. Bridget (1990) | Lawson-Gould | Klein Forest High School: Houston, TX

59. Let Praises Ring (1990) | Unpublished | Abington Press: Nashville

60. Three Challenges (1990) | Lawson-Gould | Kilgore College Choral: Kilgore, TX

61. A Carol for Commitment (1990) | Augsburg | Canyon Creek Presbyterian Church: Richardson, TX

62. Two Blake Songs (1990) | Lawson-Gould | Lyons Township HS: Western Springs, IL

63. The Tabernacle of God (1990) | H.W. Gray/Belwin | Roswell UMC: Roswell, GA

64. A Carol for Easter (1991) | Augsburg | Spring Valley UMC: Dallas, TX

65. Christ Loves the Church (1991) | Unpublished | United Methodist Church: Montesano, WA

66. A Carol of Thanksgiving (1991) | Augsburg | First Presbyterian Church: Norman, OK

67. Keep My Commandments (1992) | AMSI | First UMC: Texarkana, AR

68. A Prayer for Singing Praises (1992) | Unpublished | Manchester UMC Chancel Choir: Manchester, MO

69. Child of the Universe (1992) | Belwin | West Heights UMC: Wichita, KS

70. Let Your Light Shine (1992) | Hope | First UMC: Richardson, TX

71. Fancy (1993) | Lawson-Gould | Robert E. Lee HS Treble Choir: Tyler, TX

72. Life Has Many Rhythms (1993) | Lawson-Gould | First UMC: Dallas, TX

73. Come, Holy Spirit (1993) | Selah | First Presbyterian Church: San Anselmo, CA

74. Glory to God (1993) | Unpublished | Polk Street UMC: Amarillo, TX

75. If You Are Risen with Christ (1993) | Hope | United Church of Christ: Yankton, SD

76. The House of God (1994) | Selah | Plymouth Park UMC: Irving, TX

77. Consecrate the Place and Day (1994) | Lawson-Gould | Thomas Jefferson HS: Cedar Rapids, IA

78. The Threefold Truth (1994) | Lawson-Gould | Community Church Choir: Honolulu, HI

79. The Devil's Nine Questions (1994) | Lawson-Gould | Los Robles Master Chorale: Moorpark, CA

80. Great Art Thou, O Lord (1994) | Lawson-Gould | Elmhurst College: Elmhurst, IL

81. My Heart (1994) | Lawson-Gould | The Palmetto Mastersingers: Columbia, SC

82. My Younger Years (1994) | Lawson-Gould | The Palmetto Mastersingers: Columbia, SC

83. My Native Land (1994) | Lawson-Gould | The Palmetto Mastersingers: Columbia, SC

84. A Day for Singing (1994) | Lawson-Gould | United Methodist Church: Westlake Village, CA

85. We Praise You, O Lord (1995) | Unpublished | Christ UMC: Tucson, AZ

86. A Prayer for the Fleet (1995) | Unpublished | US Navy Seachanters: Washington, DC

87. Sea Fever (1996) | Unpublished | US Navy Seachanters: Washington, DC

88. Into Your Hands, O Lord (1996) | Lawson-Gould | The Roman Catholic Diocese: Youngstown, OH

89. Let All the World Sing (1996) | Lawson-Gould | NC Education Association All-State Choir: Winston-Salem

90. Constant Commitment (1996) | Unpublished | Bellaire UMC: Bellaire, TX

91. This is My Native Land (1997) | Lawson-Gould | Richardson ISD: Richardson, TX

92. We Will Praise the Lord (1998) | Kjos Music | Christ UMC: Tucson, AZ

Appendix G

36 Years of Service to America's Youth

A Partial List of Choral Festivals for High Schools, Churches and Colleges (All-State, Regional, District and Denominational) Conducted by Lloyd Pfautsch

1959 Florida MENC All-State Choir (Tampa)

1962 Arkansas High School Choral Festival (Hot Springs)

1963 Presbyterian Church Music Conference Youth Choir (Montreat, NC)

1963 Iowa MENC All-State Choir (Des Moines)

1963 Nebraska MENC All-State Choral Clinic (Kearney)

1963 Texas Music Educator's Association (MEA) Region 5 Choir (Houston)

1963 Texas MEA Region 7 Choir (Corpus Christi)

1964 Arkansas High School Choral Festival (Hot Springs)

1964 Texas MEA Region 10 (Arlington)

1965 Oklahoma Methodists Youth Choir Festival (Oklahoma City)

1965 Texas MEA Region 10 Choral Festival (Grand Prairie)

1965 Tucson (AZ) All-City High School Choral Festival

1965 Lincoln (NB) All-City Junior and Senior High School Choral Festival

1966 37th Annual Fox Valley Music Festival (Aurora, IL) – 1100 in the choir

1967 Colorado All-State Choir (University of Denver) – 323 singers from 101 Schools

1968 Omaha 19th Annual All-City Choral Festival – 500 in choir

1968 Chicago All-City Choir Festival

1968 Conducted 23rd Annual New Mexico Music Educator's Association All-State Choir

1968 University of the Pacific Summer Music Camp (Stockton, CA) – Chapel and Concert Choirs

1968 Chadron State College (NB) 10th Annual Summer Fine Arts Festival

1968 North Carolina MEA All-State Choir (Greensboro)

1968 University of Kansas 31st Annual Midwestern Music and Arts Camp

1969 Illinois MEA All-State Choir (Peoria)

1969 Manitoba MEA (Canada) 9th Annual January Workshop

1969 South Dakota MEA All-State Choir (Sioux Falls)

1970 Arkansas MEA All-State Choir (Little Rock)

1970 Indiana MEA All-State Choir

1970 Southwestern State College (Weatherford, OK) 20th Annual Senior High Choral Festival

1970 Dallas ISD "Orbit" Concerts to Promote Arts in Dallas Schools

1970 Texas MEA, Region III (Richardson)

1970 Bemidji State College (MN) Summer Music Camp: Choir of 75 women and 16 men. Also included Band, Orchestra, Drum Majors, Baton Twirlers and Cheerleaders

1971 TX MEA Region III Choir (Dallas)

1971 10th Annual Youth Choir Rally, SW Texas Conference of UMC (Brownsville)

1971–75 Colorado State University (Fort Collins) Summer Music Camp

1971 Gulf State High School Choral Clinic (New Orleans)

1971–74 Pacific University (Forest Grove, OR) Choir Festival

1971–75 Colorado State University (Fort Collins) 10th-14th Annual Summer Music Camps

1971–72 University of the Pacific Annual Music Clinic Chorus (Stockton, CA)

1975 MENC All-Northwest Division Choir Festival (Spokane, WA)

1978 Georgia All-College Chorus (GA State University)

1978 Massachusetts All State Chorus (Amhurst)

1978 Texas MEA Region III Choir (Dallas)

1978 Indiana MEA/ADCA All-State Honors Choir

1979 Illinois MEA Division VII College Choir Festival (Evanston)

1980 Washington MEA All-State Choir (Bellingham)

1981 Roanoke College H.S. Choral Festival (Salem, VA)

1981 North Carolina Honors Choir (NCMEA; Winston-Salem)

1982 8th Annual Wentzville, MO Choral Festival (6 Community Choruses)

1982 Kennesaw College All-Star High School Choral Festival (Marietta, GA)

1983 Fairfax County, VA High School Choral Festival

1983 Louisiana All-State Choir (Baton Rouge)

1984 Illinois Honor Choir (IMEA) Springfield

1988 Texas MEA Region XX Choir (Dallas)

1993 Maryland MEA All-State Choir (Ocean City)

1994 Texas MEA Region II Choir (Wichita Falls)

1995 Oklahoma MEA Intercollegiate Honors Choir (Tulsa)

Appendix H

MM Choral Conducting Graduates With Doctorates

Name	Bachelor's Degree	Doctoral Degree	Job
Barr, Wayne	Westminster Choir Coll.	U. of Michigan	2
Bigger, William	Illinois Wesleyan Univ.	U. of Iowa	1
Byrom, Edward	West Virginia Wesleyan	Eastman School/ Music	1
Carroll, William	Millsaps College	U. of Cincinnati	1
Carnine, Albert	Illinois Wesleyan Univ.	U. of Texas	1
Cox, Christine	Indiana U.	Michigan State U.	3
Dowdy, Paul	Trinity U.	U. of Iowa	*
Engbrecht, Henry	Bethel College	U. of Cincinnati	1
Friese, Gary	U. of Brandon (Canada)	U. of Cincinnati	1
Epp, Gary	Bethel College	U. of Missouri-K.C.	3
Faulkner, Quentin	Westminster Choir Coll.	Union Theol. Seminary	1
Gladstone, Bruce	West Virginia Wesleyan	U. of Illinois	1
Hayward, Carl	Norfolk State U.	U. of Southern California	1

Hurstad, Linda	U. of Nebraska	U. of Texas	
Karna, Duane R.	U. of Puget Sound	U. of Arizona	
Kennaston, Karen	West Virginia Wesleyan	U. of North Texas	
Lofgren, Ron	Bethany College	U. of Kansas	
MacNeil, Roger	Hastings College	U. of Northern Colorado	1
Miller, Thomas E.	Biola University	U. of Southern California	1
Ostergren, Eduardo	U. of Sao Paulo (Brazil)	U. of Indiana	4
O'Neal, Roger	U. of North Texas	U. of Texas	
Parsons, Larry	Kansas Wesleyan U.	U. of Illinois	1
Pohlenz, Michael	Friends University	U. of Oklahoma	
Reeves, Anthony	U. of N.C.-Greensboro	U. of Arizona	
Regier, Marvin	U. of Manitoba (Canada)	U. of Oregon	5
Sanches, Diana	Trinity U.	U. of Texas	2
Suanders, Mary N.	Pfeiffer College	U. of Indiana	*
Schellenberg, Henry	U. of Manitoba (Canada)	U. of Iowa	1
Sneed, Bonnie Borshay	Furman U.	Michigan State U.	1
Sotherden, Ann	SUNY - Fredonia	U. of Texas	1
Ulrich, Jerry	Eastern Illinois U.	U. of Cincinnati	1
Willis, Dawn	MacMurray U.	Arizona State U.	1
Wilson, Betty K.	MacMurray U.	Boston U.	1
Wood, Gary	Principia College	U. of Illinois	1

Legend

1 - University or College　2 - Church　3 – High School
4 - Symphony Conductor　5 - Professional Singer　* - Deceased

Appendix I

Other MM Choral Conducting Graduates

Abel, Timothy 2
Bailey, Gretchen 2
Baker, Mary Jane 10
Baker, Philip 2
Barbier, Cynthia 10
Bentley, Brian 2
Bone, David 9
Burnette, Anne 2,11
Candalaria, Idelia 10
Carr, Sarah 10
Catchings, Billy 7
Childs, Kim 8
Christiani, David 8
Cobb, Lee Anne 2
Collett, David 2
Collins, Jane 10
Daniels, Dale 2
Davis, Robert 2
Dejarnett, Douglas 2
Easter, Hal 10
Effler, Dana 2
Eison, George 2,8
Epperly, Susan 10
Fairborn, Tanya 2
Farmer, Floyd 10
Fisher, Peggy 10
Gardner, Don 2
Gruber, Rebecca 1
Henry, David 2
Huang, Jui-ying 10
Huckaby, William 4
Hutton, John 2

Jackson, Max 10
Kazee, John 2
Longhurst, Christine 2, 1
Lyton, James 10
Mathia, Catherine 11
Paguio, Reynaldo 1
Paterson, David 12
Poettker, John 11
Price, Karen 11
Purdin, Karen 10
Rhyne, Andrae 11
Simmons, Nancy 10
Smith, Sherry 10
Stevens, Steve 6
Streiff, Gary 2
Suwaki, Mitzikkazu 6
Syemen, James 1
Tucker, Dennis 2
Werner Jane 2
Wyrick, Ginger 11, 2

Kaufmann, Ron 2
Lofgren, Ron 10
Lundberg, Paul 8
Marshall, Jane 5
Nott, Cynthia 6
Parisi, James 12
Peters, Henry 2
Porter, Joseph 10
Pritchett, Billy 2
Redman, Roy 2,3
Riehle, Kevin 2
Simpson, Alan 10
Smith, Randal 10
Stewart, Carol 2
Sumner, Mark 11
Swindler, Jane 10
Thornton, Mary Jane 2
Vacca, Gary 10
Wingrove, Amy 2

Legend

1-College, University	2-Church	3-Organ Builder
4-Professional Coach	5-Composer	6-Professional Conductor
7-Theater	8-Professional Singer	9-Music Editor
10-Unknown	11-Music Educator	12-Deceased

Appendix J

An Analysis of Careers for MM Choral Conducting Graduates

Careers for MM Choral Conducting Graduates 71

College or University Positions: 5

Church Music Positions: 30

Organ-builder: 1

Professional Coach/Accompanist 1

Composer (primary employment) 1

Professional Conductor 3

Theatrical Employment 1

Professional Singer 4

Music Editor 1

Unknown 20

Music Educator 7

Deceased 2

Total Number of MM's with Doctoral Degrees: 34

College or University Positions: 18

Church Music Positions: 3

Music Editor: 1

Symphony Conductor : 1

Professional Singer: 1

Unknown: 8

Deceased: 2

Total Number of MM Choral Conducting Graduates: 105

Legend

1-College, University	2-Church	3-Organ Builder
4-Professional Coach	5-Composer	6-Professional Conductor
7-Theater	8-Professional Singer	9-Music Editor
10-Unkown	11-Music Educator	12-Deceased

Appendix K

Meditation on Psalm 67

Delivered as a Tribute to Lloyd Pfautsch at a Psalm Service Celebrating His Life and Music

Perkins Chapel, 10 October 1991

Southern Methodist University (Dallas)

To the Chief Musician: with stringed instruments. A Psalm. A Song.

May God be gracious to us and bless us and make his face to shine upon us. (*selah)*

That your way may be known upon earth, your saving power among all nations.

Let the peoples praise you, O God; let all the peoples praise you.

Let the nations be glad and sing for joy, for you judge the peoples with equity and guide the nations upon Earth. (*selah)*

Let the peoples praise you, O God; let all the peoples praise you.

The earth has yielded us increase: God, our God, has blessed us. May God continue to bless us: let all the ends of the earth revere God.

Psalm 67, a community thanksgiving for use in worship at the autumn harvest time, reflects many of the features of the Psalms as a whole and, as such, could not be more appropriate to tonight's occasion. This is the time of the autumn harvest, for one thing, and we are here to give thanks to God, in this case for a Chief Musician, for another. It is also one of the Psalms Martin Luther considered important enough to set metrically for regular use as a chorale, and one that J. S. Bach used for *Cantata 69*. Further, it is one of the few Psalms left that Lloyd Pfautsch has not set to music—yet!

We know by the ascription to this psalm that it is addressed to the Chief Musician, the leader. It was to be performed by the leader with the refrain done either by the choir, as we just did, or by the congregation. We also believe that the two places marked "*selah*" refer to instrumental interludes, hence Mary Vogelson's beautiful and fitting accompaniment on the small harp. We are not attempting total authenticity here, of course, but the ascription does tell the leader that this Psalm is to be performed with stringed instruments, probably by a *Zammarin*: a choir singing with plucked instruments for accompaniment. It is further ascribed as "a Psalm," meaning a poem to be sung (or at least intoned) and also as "a Song," meaning it is to be rendered to music. Eric Routley, in his book *Exploring the Psalms* points out that in many respects the Psalter can be regarded as a collection of hymns. However, it was not a hymnbook in our modern sense, in that only the chief musician needed a copy since the congregation's participation was limited to refrains, such as the one we just heard, and to songs that everyone knew by heart. The rest was done by the leader or Chief Musician and the trained choir, who also played instruments. For the average person in the early congregation, the Psalms were more to be heard than participated in.

We read in I Chronicles 15:22 that at the building of the Second Temple, David organized the musicians, even before the Ark was brought forth. He placed Chenaniah in charge, as a leader of the Levites in music, because he "understood music." Cheneniah was the Chief Musician of his tribe. Tonight we are here first to praise God with Psalms for the many blessings we have received, but second to honor a chief musician, one among us who knows the songs of the people and the Scriptures, and who understands music: **Dr. Lloyd Pfautsch.**

Psalm 67 makes very clear from the opening with its cultic reference to the Aaronic Blessing: "May God be gracious to us and bless us," that thanks to God for guidance and saving powers is the main purpose of the Psalm. The more selfish and worldly matter of gathering to give thanks for a successful harvest, which meets one's temporal, earthly needs and pleasures is merely of secondary consideration.

My esteemed and beloved colleague, Roger Deschner, was to have been here presenting this meditation in a far more witty and wonderful way than I could possibly achieve. Lloyd, and the Lord, know that Roger would be here if the choice were his.

When I spoke to Mary Vogelson about playing for this service, I explained that I was giving a meditation and not a sermon. "What's the difference?" she asked. I responded that a meditation is usually shorter and doesn't have to accomplish anything. So, naturally I feel more at home with a meditation!

But back to Roger Deschner. He recently wrote a short book for the General Board of Discipleship of the United Methodist Church entitled: *Your Ministry of Singing in the Church Choir*. The first chapter is a fascinating discussion on the role of the chief musician in the Hebraic tradition. Roger points out that after the fall of the First Temple, the people gathered, without the benefit of their scrolls, in small congregations or synagogues. The leader, who was later known as the *shelliach sibbur*, was chosen as the one among them who: "had music in him and who knew the scriptures and songs." He was both the teacher and the song leader. Later, as the tradition evolved, these two functions were separated and the *rabbi* became the teacher of the Word and the *chazzan* became the leader of the music. They were, I hasten to add, equal in status, respect, importance and, no doubt, salary and fringe benefits! The latter is a concept that the American Guild of Organists, the American Choral Directors Association and the denominational musicians fellowships have dedicated many of their waking hours trying to re-establish in our own day. No wonder Master of Sacred Music students love the *Old Testament* while the Master of Divinity students usually relate more strongly to the *New Testament*!

Had Lloyd Pfautsch lived in the days following the end of the First Temple, he would undoubtedly have been a *shelliach sibbur* or at the Second Temple, a *chazzan*, for he knows the Scriptures and understands music.

In 1958, the faculty and administration of Southern Methodist University made one of their very best decisions when they offered a contract to a booming-bass-voiced choral director from Illinois Wesleyan University to come here and establish a Master of Sacred Music degree program. Lloyd wisely spent his first year meeting, negotiating with, and haranguing the faculties of the Music School and the School of Theology until a degree program, not unlike the one he had experienced at Union Theological Seminary in New York City, could be established. With significant financial assistance from Jake and Nita Akin of Wichita Falls, he established the MSM program and directed it for the next six years. Later, a bequest from Harold and Lucy Cabe allowed the program to rise to still higher levels of distinction, funding tonight's program, for example. What developed is a Sacred Music program in a seminary setting that has been able to train and nourish *chazzans*, musicians to lead the people's song with understanding of both the Scriptures and the music. Because of these graduates there are such leaders in churches and schools throughout the United States and in many other countries as well.

Beyond this significant accomplishment and many more listed in your program, and beyond all of the other feats in the staggeringly impressive list of Lloyd Pfautsch's achievements as singer, teacher, composer and conductor, shines one pervasive truth—he is a man of God! As such he knows, like the psalmist, that to come before God means to praise God with thanksgiving. God is, as Arthur Weiser points out in his book *The Psalms*, the one who is the first to give thanks. So, in giving thanks to God we all, all nations as the psalmists says, meet in a great congregation united by our common obligation to God. Or, as Eric Routley sums up the meaning of *Psalm 67*: "The secret of peace with nature is peace with God."

In saying thank you to Lloyd Pfautsch for his great gifts to us, we frame that gratitude in the greater thanks to God for God's gifts to us all, including those given to God's servant, Lloyd. With the writer of Psalm 67, we look to the future with hope and assurance as we read:

God, our God has blessed us.
May God continue to bless us.
Let all the ends of the earth revere God. Amen.

Kenneth W. Hart, DMA

Appendix L

Lloyd Pfautsch Remembered: A Eulogy

I first met Lloyd Pfautsch when I came to Southern Methodist University to audition for my current position. He quickly invited me to attend his University Chorale rehearsal and then to chat afterwards. When I entered rehearsal he had just finished warm-ups and stopped to introduce me to the choir. They proceeded on cue to give a single handclap, which he called "an applau," the imagined singular form of the word "applause." This must have been a frequent trick, but the choir still enjoyed doing it and I was highly amused. Here was a conductor who practiced what he preached in his books. He valued human relations, his choral gestures were expressive, but disciplined and clear, and he most certainly made regular use of humor in rehearsals.

Pfautsch was born September 21, 1921, in Washington, Missouri (near St. Louis). He received a Bachelors degree from Elmhurst College in 1943. Planning to follow his parents' hopes, he anticipated becoming a minister in the Evangelical and Reform tradition when he entered New York City's Union Theological Seminary that fall. His musical career flourished. He was soloist at Brick Presbyterian Church under Clarence and Helen Dickinson and sang in Toscanini's NBC Symphony Chorus. He made several recordings and also met his future wife, Edith Herseth, who sang under Toscanini, too, at the time. The year 1946 was significant for Pfautsch. He graduated from Union with a Bachelor of Divinity, he decided he wanted a musical career instead of a ministerial one and entered the Master of Sacred Music program at Union and he also married Edith Herseth! All of the above changed his life for the better. He remained grateful for all of these important events until his death on October 3, 2003.

No matter how you look at it, the word "prolific" describes Lloyd Pfautsch. He published nearly 300 compositions (72 of which were commissions) with 34 different publishers; he was guest lecturer at more than 50 colleges and universities in the U.S. and abroad; he graduated 104 students with the MM in Choral Conducting, 34 of whom later received doctorates; and he conducted countless All-State Honor Choruses and multi-church festival choirs throughout the country. His impact on choral music in the U.S. and beyond was pervasive for the second half of the 20th Century. It persists today as dozens of his graduates hold important academic and church choral positions around the world. That influence also continues in the performance of his music throughout much of the Western world. When the repertoires for the All-State Choruses in the U.S. appear each spring in *The Choral Journal*, there are always Pfautsch pieces on the lists.

No one in recent memory has been more dedicated to the choral art than Lloyd Pfautsch. He began singing in public at age 3 and joined ensembles as early as anyone would let him. He was fortunate to make the acquaintance of Robert Shaw as Shaw was rising to the position of the foremost choral conductor in America. He sang on most of the early Shaw recordings, including the best-selling first Christmas album and achieved the status of colleague and friend with the maestro. Shaw remained fiercely loyal to Pfautsch and continued to help him professionally until his own death. It was Shaw who recommended Lloyd as the choral conductor for the 1965 twentieth anniversary celebration of the United Nations in San Francisco. The Convocation of Religion for World Peace was held at the San Francisco Cow Palace on the last night of the anniversary proceedings. The group brought together leaders of 7 of the world's largest religions (Catholic, Protestant, Jew, Hindu, Buddhist, Moslem and Eastern Orthodox) to worship with a common cause: world peace. Secretary-General U Thant spoke at the culminating worship service and so most of the distinguished delegates to the U.N. attended. Pfautsch conducted a large brass ensemble and a choir of 2000, mostly from the Bay area. They rehearsed for three days prior to their public appearance. The event earned Pfautsch much praise and many accolades that continued for months afterwards. It was, to him, a seminal event in his career and one of his fondest memories.

Two universities were fortunate to benefit from many years of Pfautsch's work and creativity: Illinois Wesleyan University (1948–58) and Southern Methodist University (1958–92). At both schools he produced nationally prominent choirs and established published series of commissioned choral works while leaving an indelible impression on the music faculties and the institutions as well. Because his career at SMU was considerably longer he was able to exercise creativity in significantly more ways there. He was brought to SMU to establish the Master of Sacred Music program, which he did most successfully. He taught at both the School of Theology and the School of Music, maintaining a faculty load that would overtax any two "normal" faculty members trying to equal it. All the while he also founded the Dallas Civic Chorus and conducted them for 25 years without stipend, found time to compose anthems on a regular basis and made time for his growing family.

After a few years he decided to work full-time in the School of Music and was chosen as the first Associate Dean for Music in the newly formed Meadows School of the Arts. While he really did not like administrative work very much he attacked it tenaciously and was able to establish a new piano pedagogy department and managed to hire his former student, Robert Anderson, to build a distinguished organ department. As the number of organ students grew he successfully made the case for building several additional organs in the School of the Arts. The organ and choral departments eventually vied for national attention and supported the Sacred Music program very effectively. Pfautsch and Anderson collaborated on many projects through the years, including the well-known annual Christmas Worship Service at Perkins Chapel. The service was created by Pfautsch and continues to be popular with the SMU and Dallas communities today.

One of his greatest innovations was development of one of the first Master of Choral Conducting programs in higher education. He pioneered in videotaping student conductors as a pedagogic device. By the same token he also produced videotape on conducting. Eventually he wrote three books as well as an important chapter in a fourth one discussing conducting and the development of choirs. Perhaps the most widely used today is his *English Diction for the Singer* (1971).

Pfautsch received many honors during his distinguished career. He was awarded honorary doctorates from Elmhurst College (Doctor of Music, 1959), Illinois Wesleyan University (Doctor of Humane Letters, 1978), and West Virginia Wesleyan University (Doctor of Humane Letters, 1985). The Board of Higher Education and Ministries of the United Methodist Church designated him their University Scholar/Teacher for 1982. At SMU he received the "M" Award (the highest award given by the university for sustained inspiration to and efforts on its behalf) and was selected the Meadows Distinguished Professor in 1984. He was granted *emeritus* status in 1992.

The Texas Choral Directors Association awarded him the Distinguished Choirmaster accolade in 1991.

Lloyd Pfautsch was an uncommon person. He was kind, modest and pastoral in his dealings with students and colleagues. He was an uncommon parent, as his children and grandchildren testified at his memorial service on October 7, 2003. He was certainly an uncommon musician. He was both a pioneer and a national leader in the teaching of choral conducting. He was also an outstanding singer in his early years and a remarkable conductor for the past half century. Those of us fortunate to have known and worked with Lloyd have been changed for the better by his warmth, his humor, his concern for humanity and his prodigious musical talent. As his daughter, Debbie, put it at the memorial service, "The heavenly choir has a new conductor now, and it's time to get the diction right!"

Kenneth Hart, Director
Graduate Program in Sacred Music
Southern Methodist University
October, 2003

Endnotes

Chapter 1

1 From the 1827 marriage record. The original document is in the Catholic Diocesan files in Bamberg (upper Franconia district).

2 See Pfautsch Family Tree, Appendix A.

3 From the website for Washington (MO) under "Historic Washington," updated 5 July 2000, and from conversations with L. Pfautsch.

4 From a taped interview with Lloyd Pfautsch in March of 2000.

5 From a taped conversation with Lloyd Pfautsch in March of 2000.

6 Linda Bernal in an undated article in a 1980 edition of *The SMU Daily Campus.*

7 From an undated column in the *Washington Missourian* , Spring of 1939, found in the high school scrapbook at the home of Lloyd Pfautsch.

8 From a concert program in one of Pfautsch's scrapbooks.

9 A photocopy of the 37th Annual Commencement at Washington High School on 19 May 1939 (in the author's files) gives the information about his accomplishments.

10 Other glee clubs chosen were from Duke University (J. Foster Barnes, Conductor), Purdue University (Albert Stewart, Conductor), University of Oklahoma (Lara Haggard, Conductor), Dartmouth College, the University of Rochester (duo-pianists Whitamore and Lowe, Conductors), University of Redlands (W. B. Olds, Conductor) and Washington and Lee University. From an undated newspaper clipping in Pfautsch's scrapbooks.

11 From an undated review by Richard D. DeYoung in what Pfautsch referred to as "The Elmhurst Newpaper."

12 This incipient talent is also observable in the 1942 work Pfautsch completed with the help of Walter Hille, *Ave verum corpus*. A copy is in the author's files.

Chapter 2

1 Unsigned article in *The Evening Monitor*, McAllen, TX, December 17, 1945.

2 Catalogue for Union Theological Seminary, 1946-47.

3 During Pfautsch's first year at Illinois Wesleyan (1948) an interview he gave to a local reporter states that *Israel at the Red Sea* was performed "several times in New

York." Dorothy Reichert, in *The Pantograph* (Bloomington, Illinois), December 1948.

4 Foss, like Shaw, was a student of Julius Herford (see *NYTimes* Obituary on 18 September 1981).

5 Pfautsch did not ever sing with the famous touring Robert Shaw Chorale, as has often been stated in print. He was invited to, but moved on with his career as that group was being formed. He sang under Robert Shaw many times for recorded and live performances, but not in the Chorale. He was hired for the RCA Victor Chorale (directed by Shaw) and for *ad hoc* recordings in NYC.

6 Among them Lukas Foss, Robert Shaw, Margaret Hillis, Roger Wagner, and Elaine Brown. See Robert Sumner's article "In Memoriam: Julius Herford" in *The Choral Journal*, December 1981: 9.

7 From a taped conversation with Young on October 23, 2000.

8 From a taped interview with Parker on July 5, 2000, in Seattle, WA.

Chapter 3

1 From a taped interview with Pfautsch in March, 2000. He soon learned that he could not adopt Shaw's style with a paid, professionally trained choir without modifying it for the university setting.

2 From a taped interview with Anderson in April 2000.

3 Unsigned review in *The Musical Courier*, 1 May 1952.

4 Dorothy Reichardt in *The Pantograph* (Bloomington, Illinois), December 1948.

5 Letter to Marjorie Farmer at Shawnee Press, Inc. dated 31 March 1955.

6 From a taped interview with Gould on June 26, 2000.

7 From a taped interview with Gould on June 26, 2000.

8 A review in *Musical America*, 15 April 1952. A quite similar positive review of the choir and the George pieces may be found in *Musical Courier*, May 1, 1952.

9 See Appendix F.

10 Paraphrase from the June 1978 issue of the *Illinois Wesleyan University Alumni Bulletin* as reprinted in the May 1979 issue of *The Choral Journal*, official magazine of the American Choral Directors Association.

11 A copy of this letter is in the author's files.

12 Vaughan Williams' 9 July 1952 letter includes the following: "As regards your kind invitation to write a piece for you, I fear my other commitments will make it impossible for me. If you want to do something by me I hope you will be able to find something that I have already written."

13 From a taped interview with Pfautsch in March 2000.

14 From a taped interview with Pfautsch in March 2000.

15 Peter Deuel, "U. of I. Festival Praised" in *The Champaign-Urbana Courier*, April 10, 1957.

16 A photocopy of the note is in the author's files. John Thaddeus is Shaw's youngest son.

17 From a taped interview with Pfautsch in March of 2000.

18 From a taped interview with Marshall on June 2, 2000.

19 From copies of Niebuhr's letters to Pfautsch, dated January 10 and 24, 1957, respectively.

Chapter 4

1 Lloyd Pfautsch, "Curriculum of Church Music of a Theological Seminary: A Historical Justification and a Formulation," Unpublished MSM Thesis, New York: Union Theological Seminary (1948).
2 From a conversation with retired Professor John Holbert, first a student at Perkins School of Theology and later a longtime faculty member, March 2000.
3 See Epilogue.
4 From a taped interview with Pfautsch in March 2000.
5 From a taped interview with Pfautsch in March 2000.
6 From a taped interview with Pfautsch in March 2000.
7 Felix R. McKnight, in *The Dallas Times Herald* for November 29, 1970, p. 34A.
8 Harry Bowman, "Despite odds . . ." in *The Dallas Morning News*, May 12, 1980, page 8C.
9 "Park Cities" column in November 14, 1990, *Dallas Morning News* under "SMU Briefs."
10 From a taped interview with Anderson in April 2000.
11 See, for example, appendices G, H, and I.
12 From a taped interview with Pfautsch in March 2000.
13 Letter from Quillian to Pfautsch dated January 12, 1992, now in this author's files.
14 Lloyd Pfautsch, *A Day for Dancing*, "Foreword," iii.
15 From a taped interview with Pfautsch in March 2000.
16 According to Pfautsch's Account Book for Royalties between April 1, 1970, and May 1, 1995, the work sold 47,467 copies and earned the composer $15,853.08 in royalties making it his best-selling work.
17 From a taped interview with Gould on June 26, 2000.
18 A copy of that advertisement is in the author's files.
19 See Olin Chism's column from the *Dallas Times Herald* for June 11, 1972.
20 Pfautsch corresponded with Diemer somewhat regularly for many years, often sending each other copies of their latest published anthems. Copies of several of her letters to Pfautsch are in this author's files. See Bibliography.
21 Letter to Pfautsch dated April 15, 1986.
22 From a taped interview with Young on October 23, 2000.
23 RTR (reviewer identified only by initials) in *Billboard Magazine*, 22 October 1988.

Chapter 5

1 See appendices B, C, and F.
2 Richard Cox (University of North Carolina-Greensville) Book Review column, page 26 in *The Choral Journal,* October 1980. The third book compared is Dorothy Uris's *To Sing in English.* For another comparison of the three "bibles" of English diction for singers, see David Larson's (Roosevelt University) book review in the December 1972 *National Association of Teachers of Singing Bulletin*, pages 33–35.
3 From a taped interview with Marshall on June 2, 2000.

4 Walter Rodby, in *The School Musician* 43, no. 4 (December 1971).
5 Letter from George Low, Music Chairman for the Convocation, on May 26, 1965. Low also mentions sending Pfautsch a recording of the earlier celebration conducted by Shaw.
6 *The San Francisco Examiner* for Friday, June 25, 1965 states that 16,000 were expected to attend. *The San Francisco Chronicle* for Monday, June 28, 1965, notes that the police present estimated that 5,000, in addition to the 2,000+ musicians, were there.
7 The invitation from Mrs. Rogers and a copy of Pfautsch's acceptance letter (dated June 22, 1965) are in the author's files.
8 Letter from Low to Pfautsch sent July 7, 1965.
9 Letter from Hairston to Pfautsch, December 29, 1982.
10 Letter from Hairston to Pfautsch, June 27, 1969.
11 From a copy of a letter sent to Pfautsch by Shaw on March 4, 1970.
12 From Shaw's inscription on Pfautsch's copy of *Dear People* sent to him by Jerry Ulrich in December of 1980.
13 This writer has photocopies of letters from these well-known musicians and others written to Pfautsch during his many years of active professional life (see Bibliography).
14 Shaw was referring to the Lawson-Gould catalogue of choral music.
15 Wagner made this statement at a Choral Workshop at Lake Geneva, New York, attended by the author in June of 1985.
16 From an email sent to this author by Robert Brooks, an alumnus of Pfautsch's SMU choirs, on March 21, 2000.
17 Ibid.
18 From an email sent to this author by Mr. Collett on June 29, 2002.
19 Quoted in Olin Chism's 11 June 1972 column in *The Dallas Times Herald.*
20 From a telephone conversation with Mr. Kravig-Williams on 25 November 2013.
21 For the list of these honorary degrees see Program: *West Virginia Wesleyan College Founders Day Program.* (October 18, 1985): 3.
22 In 1984 Pfautsch was given a "Citation for Pastoral Service" from the United Church of Christ on the occasion of the twenty-fifth anniversary of his ordination. The signed certificate, dated 26 May 1984, is in this author's files.

Epilogue

1 Carolyn Cabela, "Program to Honor Pfautsch" in the April 28, 1992, *The Daily Campus*: 5.
2 Copies of this note and several other letters from Routley are in this author's files.
3 Edith Pfautsch died on October 25, 2011. A well-attended memorial service for her was held in Dallas on August 26, 2012.

Bibliography

Books

Adler, Kurt. *Phonetics and Diction in Singing: Italian, French, Spanish, German.* Minneapolis: University of Minnesota Press, 1967.

Chase, Gilbert. *America's Music from the Pilgrims to the Present.* Rev. 2nd ed. New York: McGraw-Hill, 1966.

Decker, Harold A. and Julius Herford. *Choral Conducting: A Symposium.* New York: Appleton-Century-Crofts, 1973.

Deschner, Roger. *Your Ministry of Singing in the Church.* Nashville, TN: Discipleship Resources, 1990.

Donington, Robert. *The Interpretation of Early Music.* 2nd ed. London: Faber and Faber, 1963.

Ehmann, Wilhelm. *Choral Directing.* Translated by George D. Wiebe. Minneapolis, MN: Augsburg, 1968.

Espina, Noni. *Vocal Solos for Protestant Services.* New York: Vita d'Arte, 1974.

Green, Elizabeth. *The Modern Conductor.* Englewood Cliffs, NJ: Prentice-Hall, 1961.

Jacobs, Arthur, ed. *Choral Music: A Symposium.* Baltimore: Penguin Books, 1963.

Marshall, Jane. *Grace Noted.* Edited by Rosemary Heffley. Carol Stream, IL: Hope Publishing Company, 1992.

Marshall, Madeleine. *The Singer's Manual of English Diction.* New York: G. Schirmer, 1963.

Mussulman, Joseph A. *Dear People/ Robert Shaw, A Biography*. Bloomington: Indiana University Press (1979).

Pfautsch, Lloyd. *Choral Therapy*. Nashville: Abingdon Press, 1994.

———. *English Diction for the Singer*. New York: Lawson-Gould, 1971.

———. *Mental Warm-ups for the Choral Director*. New York: Lawson-Gould, 1969.

Rice, William C. *A Concise History of Church Music.* New York: Abingdon Press, 1964.

Rice, William C., and Austin Lovelace. *Music and Worship in the Church.* New York: Abingdon Press, 1976.

Routley, Eric. *The Church and Music.* London: Gerald Duckworth, 1967.

———. *Twentieth Century Church Music.* London: Herbert Jenkins, 1964.

Stevenson, Robert. *Protestant Church Music in America.* New York: W. W. Norton & Co., 1966.

Terrien, Samuel. *The Psalms and Their Meaning for Today: Their Original Purposes, Contents, Religious Truth, Poetic Beauty and Significance.* Indianapolis, IN: Bobbs-Merrill, 1952.

Uris, Dorothy. *To Sing in English: A Guide to Improved Diction.* London: Boosey & Hawkes, 1971.

Weiser, Artur. *The Psalms.* Translated by Herbert Hartwell. Philadelphia: The Westminster Press, 1962.

Werner, Jack. *Mendelssohn's "Elijah": A Historical and Analytical Guide to the Oratorio.* London: Chappell, 1965.

Young, Percy. *The Choral Tradition.* New York: W. W. Norton, 1971.

Magazine and Newspaper Articles

Advertisement for St. Bartholomew's Episcopal Church Christmas Services. *New York Times*, December 23, 1973.

"Anthem Notes." *Journal of Church Music.* June 1986, 15–16.

Bernal, Linda. "Choral Director Enjoys Talking, Too." *Dallas Morning News,* 1980.

Boody, Charles G. "Book Review." *Choral Journal*, February 1972, 21–22.

Bowman, Harry. "Despite Odds, Chorus Keeps Singing." *Dallas Morning News,* May 12, 1980: 8C.

Cabela, Carolyn. "Program to Honor Pfautsch." *Daily Campus* (SMU), April 28, 1992, 5.

Cantrell, Scott. "Obituary: Lloyd Pfautsch." *Dallas Morning News*, October 4, 2003: 4B.

———. "Lloyd Pfautsch Choral Master." *Dallas Morning News*, October 12, 2003.

Chism, Olin. "Civic Chorus Performs." *Dallas Times Herald* (undated).

———. "10 Years Marked By Civic Chorus." *Dallas Times Herald,* May 14, 1970.

———. "Dignified Pfautsch Banned in Richmond." *Dallas Times Herald,* June 11, 1972.

"Churches to Mark Anniversaries." *Dallas Morning News,* September 15, 1984:50a.

"Concert Set at University: Robert Shaw Will Be Guest Conductor." *Champaign-Urbana Courier*, April 10, 1957.

Cox, Richard. "Book Review." *Choral Journal*, October 1980: 26

Dalton, Sydney. "Cantata Here." *Nashville Banner*, November 26, 1962.

Deuel, Peter. "U. of I. Festival Praised." *Champaign-Urbana Courier* (undated).

DeYoung, Richard. "Large, Appreciative Audience Hears College Spring Concert." Unidentified Elmhurst, Illinois newspaper, Spring 1942.

"Dr. Lloyd Pfautsch Commemorates 25th Anniversary of Collegiate Choir Commission Series on Founder's Day." *Choral Journal,* May 1978: 30-32. Reprinted from *Illinois Wesleyan University Alumni Bulletin,* June 1978.

"Emotional Maestro." *Champaign-Urbana Courier*, December 14, 1956: 23.

Goad, Kimberly. "Dr. Lloyd Pfautsch." *Dallas Morning News*, May 24, 1992: 5J.

Haacke, Lorraine. "Dance in Review: 'Befana,' 'Carols' " *Dallas Times-Herald*, December 5, 1975.

Herrington, Jeff. "Pfautsch: His Music, His Musings." *The Mustang*, Spring 1980: 17-19.

Hodges, Dolores "Conductor Shaw at UI; Rehearses for Concert" *News-Gazette* Champaign-Urbana, ? 1957.

"Illinois Wesleyan Choir in Concert" *Musical Courier,* May 1, 1952.

Larson, David. "Guest Book Review: 'To Sing in English and 'English Diction for the Singer'" *The NATS Bulletin,* December 1972: 33-35.

Lewis, Eugene. "A 'Messiah' of Brilliance." *The Dallas Times-Herald,* December 20, 1965.

McKnight, Felix R. "Dallas Civic Chorus Thrills the Millions." *Dallas Times Herald,* November 29, 1970, p. 34A.

"Musician's Role Is Just About Total Involvement" *SMU NOW,* SMU Information Services (undated).

Nicholas, Louis. "Blair Quartet Delivers Spirited Performance" *Nashville Tennessean*, Spring 1960.

Nicholas, Louis. "Junior Choirs Premiere Christmas Cantata Here" *Nashville Tennessean*, November 26, 1962.

"1977 ACDA National Convention." *The Choral Journal,* December 1976: 18-21.

Perkins, Franklin E. "Big 12 Music Festival" *Illinois State Journal-Register* (undated).

Pfautsch, Lloyd. "A New Response to an Ageless Commission" *Perkins School of Theology Journal* 11-12, Spring 1959: 18-21.

Pfautsch, Lloyd. "Sing Us No Sad Songs" *Pan Pipes of Sigma Alpha Iota* (undated): 17-19.

"Playwright Named Dean; Pfautsch is Associate of New School of Arts" *SMU Campus,* March 20, 1964: 1, 6.

Reichardt, Dorothy. "Review" *Pantograph,* Bloomington, IL, December 1948.

Rodby, Walter. "New Pfautsch Christmas Cantata" *School Musician,* ?, 1962.

Rodby, Walter. "New Things – Nice Things" *School Musician* 43, no.4 (December 1971).

Rosenfield, John. "Messiah Has Refound Numbers." *Dallas Morning News*, December 20, 1965.

RTR. "Video Review: 'Coming Alive!' *Billboard,* October 22, 1988: 71.

"16,000 Expected at Rally of Faith," *San Francisco Examiner*, June 25, 1965: 14.

"SMU Recital." *Dallas Morning News: "Park Cities,"* December 14, 1990: 3K.

Sumner, Robert. "In Memoriam: Julius Herford" *Choral Journal,* December 1981: 9.

Underwood, W. T. "Messiah Wins Huge Ovation." *Wichita Falls Record News*, December 11, 1958.

Waite, Elmont. "The World's Faiths Praise U.N.'s Quest." *San Francisco Chronicle*, June 28, 1965: 1.

Weber, Victor. "Book Review: 'Choral Conducting: A Symposium.'" *Choral Journal,* February 1974: 16-17.

"World Faiths – United on U.N. Goal" *San Francisco Chronicle*, June 28, 1965:13.

Young, Carlton. "Composing for the Parish Choir" *Journal of Church Music,* February 1970: 42-45.

Personal Letters in Author's Files

Copland, Aaron. Letter to Pfautsch, November 19, 1952.

Dickinson, Helen and Clarence. Letter to Pfautsch, August 6, 1948.

Diemer, Emma Lou. Letters to Pfautsch, June 10, 1974; August 6, 1975; November 24, 1976; December 14, 1975; March 4, 1977; April 15, 1977; March 2, 1978 and April 16,1986.

Donnington, Robert, OBE. Letter to Pfautsch, August 3, 1983.

George, Earl. Letters to Pfautsch, October 26, 1977; April 2, 1978; and April 27, 1993.

Green, Fred Pratt. Letters to Pfautsch, September 28, 1978; November 12, 1979; December 3, 1979; May 23, 1985; January 2, 1986; June 9, 1986; July 15, 1988; December 8, 1988; March 12, 1989; June 8, 1980 and August 28, 1990.

Hairston, Jester. Letters to Pfautsch, June 27, 1969; September 19, 1969; May 16, 1970; August 2, 1977; December 29, 1982; August 29, 1987; July 27, 1989 and March 20,1991.

Herford, Julius. Letters to Pfautsch, September 19, 1954 and February 10, 1969.

Hogg, W. Richey (SMU Theology Professor). Letter to Pfautsch, December 18, 1959.

Low, George W. Letters to Pfautsch, April 22, 1965; May 16, 1965; May 27, 1965, and July 7, 1965.

Mathias, William, OBE. Letter to Pfautsch, October 30, 1990.

Mechem, Kirk. Letters to Pfautsch, August 14, 1991; December 5, 1992; March 7, 1994 and April 16, 1994.

Milner, Anthony. Letter to Pfautsch, July 17, 1978.

Lockwood, Normand. Letter to Marjorie Farmer of Shawnee Press, March 31, 1955.

Neibuhr, Reinhold. Letters to Pfautsch, January 10, 1957 and January 24, 1957.

Nystedt, Knut. Letter to Pfautsch, April 3, 1977.

Ogden, Schubert (SMU Theology Professor). Letter to Pfautsch, November 26, 1960.

Peeters, Flor. Letter to Pfautsch, February 7, 1957.

Pfautsch, Lloyd. Letter to Dr. and Mrs. William Lister Rogers, June 22, 1965.

Pfautsch, Lloyd. Letter to Earl George, April 23, 1993.

Pfautsch, Lloyd. Letters to Kenneth Hart, May 1992 and March 8, 2001.

Pfautsch, Lloyd. Letters to George W. Low, February 4, 1965; June 17, 1965 and one undated.

Phillips, Burrill. Letter to Pfautsch, December 2, 1959.

Quillian, Joseph D., Jr. (SMU Theology Dean). Letters to Pfautsch, December 20, 1966; December 18, 1978 and January 12, 1992.

Routley, Erik. Letters to Pfautsch, May 8, 1971; September 30, 1975; November 20, 1975; May 11, 1977; October 12, 1978; November 20, 1978; August 18, 1979 and September 24, 1979.

Rutter, Sir John. Letter to Pfautsch, November 12, 19??.

Shaw, Robert Lawson. Letters to Pfautsch, May 6, 1957; March 4, 1970 and February 28, 1985.

Vaughan Williams, Ralph. Letter to Pfautsch, July 9, 1952.

Willcocks, Sir David. Letter to Pfautsch, January 18, 1977.

Williamson, Malcolm, CBE. Letters to Pfautsch, June 13, 1975; August 8, 1975 and one undated.

Wright, A. A. (California Choral Conductors' Guild). Letter to Pfautsch, June 11, 1965.

Zimmerman, Heinz Werner. Letters to Pfautsch, August 15, 1975; January 29, 1985; January 29, 1985; August 7, 199? and June 5, 199?.

Miscellaneous Sources (Unless otherwise noted, in Author's Files)

Brooks, Robert. Email to Kenneth Hart, March 22, 2000.

Brooks, Robert. Email to Kenneth Hart, April 24, 2000.

Brooks, Robert. Email to Dr. Ken Hart, December 10, 2001.

Citation for Pastoral Service: Lloyd Pfautsch. United Church of Christ, May 26, 1984.

Collett, David. Email to Ken Hart, June 29, 2002.

Invitation*: Dr. and Mrs. William Lister Rogers cordially invite Dr. and Mrs. Lloyd Pfautsch to dinner*. San Francisco, CA (June 27, 1965).

Kravig-Williams, Kenton. Telephone conversation with author, November 25, 2013.

Manuscript. *There's a Little Wheel A-turnin' in my Heart* (undated)

Marriage record for Joseph Pfautsch and Martina Hoemann. Archiv des Erzbistums Bamberg, October 2, 1827, Meineck, Germany.

Miller, Thomas Edward. "The Sacred Music of Lloyd Alvin Pfautsch." DMA Dissertation. Los Angeles: University of Southern California, 1981.

Pfautsch, Debra. "Lloyd Pfautsch: A Daughter's Perspective." Eulogy delivered at the first memorial service for Pfautsch (October 7, 2003).

Pfautsch, Lloyd A. Accounting records of royalties received on his publications. November 1, 1952 through May 1, 1995, 251 pages.

Pfautsch, Lloyd A. "Curriculum of Church Music of a Theological Seminary:

A Historical Justification and a Formulation." MSM Thesis. New York: Union Theological Seminary, 1948.

Pfautsch, Lloyd A. "There's a Little Wheel A-turnin' in My Heart." Unpublished TTBB manuscript dedicated to Alfred Greenfield (Pfautsch's conducting professor at Union Theological Seminary) and his NYU Men's Glee Club.

Pfautsch, Lloyd A. "Thy Temple Stands to Serve." Written for the dedication of the new St. Peter's Evangelical and Reformed Church, Champaign-Urbana (1957).

Program: A Celebration of the Life and Musical Legacy of Lloyd Pfautsch (1921–2003). SMU's Perkins Chapel (November 14, 2003).

Program: A Celebration of the Life of Lloyd Pfautsch. Preston Hollow Presbyterian Church (October 7, 2003).

Program: Choral Program by the Summer Session Chorus. Union Theological Seminary (August 11, 1959).

Program: Dedication: St. Peter's Evangelical and Reformed Church. Champaign-Urbana, IL (November 17, 1957).

Program: A Festival of Psalms, A Service in Honor of the Music and Career of Lloyd Pfautsch. SMU's Perkins Chapel (October 10, 1991).

Program: Dallas Civic Chorus Spring Choral Concert. SMU's McFarlin Auditorium (May 19, 1962).

Program: *King David* by Arthur Honegger. McFarlin Auditorium (October 16, 1966).

Program: Niebuhr Monument Dedication. Elmhurst College, IL (May 29, 1997).

Program: Pfautsch Pfestival. Lovers Lane United Methodist Church, Dallas, TX (May 17, 1992).

Program: A Service of Celebration and Thanksgiving In Honor of the Fiftieth Anniversary Observance of the Multiple Choir Program at Second Presbyterian Church. Bloomington, IL. (May 24, 1987).

Program: SMU Choral Union. Caruth Auditorium (November 6, 1990).

Program: SMU Faculty Recital. Student Center Ballroom (December 16, 1964).

Program: SMU Faculty Recital. Caruth Auditorium (December 12, 1966).

Program: *The Messiah* by George Frederick Handel. First Methodist Church of McAllen, TX (December 16, 1945).

Program: Thirty-Seventh Annual Commencement. Washington (MO.) High School (May 19, 1939).

Program: We Gather Together: A Celebration of the Lives of Jane Marshall and Lloyd Pfautsch. First United Methodist Church of Dallas, TX (October 22, 2000).

Program: West Virginia Wesleyan College Founders Day Convocation. Buckhannon, WV (October 18, 1985).

Program: Workshop for Choral Directors. University of Wichita, KS. (June 10-14, 1963).

Shaw, Robert Lawson. Inscription on Pfautsch's copy of Joseph A. Musselman's 1977 book: *Dear People* (December 1980).

Thompson, Randall. Inscription on Pfautsch's copy of the score to Thompson's anthem *Alleluia* (February 2, 1980).

Website: www.washmo.org "Welcome to Washington!" (updated 5 July 2000).

Index